CIVIL WAR TIMES IN ST. AUGUSTINE

Jacqueline K. Fretwell, editor

Originally appeared as Volume Twenty-Three
of
EL ESCRIBANO
The St. Augustine Journal of History
The St. Augustine Historical Society

Reprinted under agreement between
The St. Augustine Historical Society
and
Florida Classics Library
Port Salerno, Florida
1988

Cover Design: James N. Baker

ISBN 0-912451-23-8

Contents

St. Augustine and the Union Blockade

George E. Buker

St. Augustine's role during two great struggles for independence was suprisingly similar. During the American Revolution St. Augustine was loyal to King George, isolated by geography from the northern centers of conflict, linked to the motherland by the royal navy at sea, protected from rebel invasion by a riverine flotilla on the St. Johns River, and secure from rebellion.[1] Almost a hundred years later during the Civil War geography and the Union navy again placed St. Augustine in the role of a loyalist center secure from revolt.

St. Augustine's geographic isolation from Northern battlefields needs no explanation, but its link to the United States awaited the Union blockade. When President Abraham Lincoln proclaimed his naval blockade of the Southern states on April 19, 1861, it was literally a paper blockade which figuratively radiated shock waves throughout the Washington Navy Department and beyond. Just over a month earlier, when Mr. Lincoln took office, the United States Navy had consisted of 76 vessels, only 42 of which were in commission. Thirty of the active service ships were absent on foreign stations and, of the remaining 12, only four were in harbors of the loyal Northern states. These four ships, carrying 25 guns and manned by 280 sailors, comprised the force immediately at hand to blockade a coastline some 3,500 miles in length, running from Alexandria, Virginia, to the Rio Grande River, and containing about 189 harbors and river mouths. Further, during the first four months of the conflict, 259 naval officers either resigned or were dismissed from the 7,600-man navy. Yet by the end of the first year the navy had constructed 52 vessels and it had purchased 136 more. The latter group contained ships of every description—whalers, fishing schooners, ferry boats, and even excursion steamers—all of which were armed, however inadequately, and put on the blockade line.[2]

The increase in vessels was matched by an increase in personnel. To augment the small regular officer corps, the secretary of the navy issued acting appointments to civilians, who were called volunteers to distinguish them from the regulars, and who came from all walks of life: rivermen, harbor pilots, and merchant marine officers. Even some of

George E. Buker is professor of history at Jacksonville University. His research in Florida military affairs has resulted in numerous articles and books including *Swamp Sailors; Sun, Sand and Water* and "The Americanization of St. Augustine" in *The Oldest City: St. Augustine, Saga of Survival.*

1. George E. Buker and Richard Apley Martin, "Governor Tonyn's Brown-Water Navy: East Florida During the American Revolution, 1775-1778," *Florida Historical Quarterly*. 58 (July 1979): 58-71.
2. "Blockade Proclamation of Abraham Lincoln, 19 April 1861," reprinted in Frank Moore, ed., *The Rebellion Record* (New York, G. P. Putnam, 1861-65), II: 78, Document 67; "Report of the Secretary of the Navy, Presented to Congress, December, 1863," reprinted in the *North American Review*, 98: 462-63.

the senior petty officers among the enlisted ratings of the navy were commissioned as volunteer officers.[3]

The Navy Department had to create a blockade organization. Initially two squadrons guarded the Confederate coastline. To the east of Key West, Florida, Flag Officer Silas H. Stringham commanded the Coast Blockading Squadron; to the west Flag Officer William Mervine directed the Gulf Blockading Squadron. Several weeks later the Coast Blockading Squadron became the Atlantic Blockading Squadron. Then in September 1861 the squadron divided into the North Atlantic Blockading Squadron, covering the coasts of Virginia and North Carolina, and the South Atlantic Blockading Squadron, whose area of concern was South Carolina, Georgia, and Florida, as far south as Cape Florida. Early in 1862 the Gulf Blockading Squadron also split into two commands; East and West Gulf Blockading Squadrons, with the dividing point just to the east of Pensacola, Florida. These four squadrons remained the navy's blockade organization throughout the war.

Horatio Bridge, chief of the Bureau of Provisions and Clothing, created the steamer force which linked the blockading vessels to Northern ports. He established a schedule so that ships standing guard over Confederate harbors could look forward to regular visits from Northern steamers bringing fresh provisions, ice, munitions, and that most essential link with home—the United States mail. Without this little noted supply system the Union navy could not have dealt so effectively with the problem of closing the South's ports and harbors.[4]

Meanwhile the Confederate government had ordered all lighthouses to be extinguished. In Florida many lighthouse keepers continued to maintain their beacons which were important aids for maritime traffic, especially along the east coast, the reefs, and keys stretching southwestward to Key West. This region long had supported a thriving wrecking and salvage industry. Yet in the early hectic days of the war these navigational aids continued to operate for the benefit of the Union navy, now assembling off the coast to initiate the blockade.

Because the lighthouse keepers were still devoted to their marine responsibilities, private individuals rose to action. Paul Arnau, customshouse officer at St. Augustine, took matters into his own hands. He organized a group known as the Coast Guard whose object was to turn off the navigational lights of Florida. They dismantled the light at St. Augustine before moving south. At Cape Canaveral they found the keepers tending the light as if nothing had happened. Arnau ran them off before removing the equipment. At Indian River he did the same to

3. Lewis R. Hamersly, *A Naval Encyclopaedia* (Philadelphia, L. R. Hamersly & Co., 1881), 569-72.
4. Charles Brandon Boynton, *The History of the Navy During the Rebellion* (New York, D. Appleton, 1867-68), 2: 80.

Joseph F. Papy before taking out vital parts to render the Jupiter Light inoperative.

Cape Florida could have been a bit more difficult, for the two lighthouse keepers there had stated many times that they would defend themselves if attacked. They stressed that their station was close enough to the shipping lanes to Key West so that their plight would be detected long before they would be compelled to surrender.

Under cover of darkness Arnau brought his men by boat from the mainland to Cape Florida. One of his men, knowing that the keepers were expecting supplies momentarily, called out that he had a message from Key West. It was a simple ruse, but both keepers came down from the tower, unbolted the iron door, and were captured by Arnau. Once in custody, they both professed loyalty to the South, but their previous action of maintaining the light beacon belied their protestations. Arnau smashed the lens before removing the lamps and burners. Mission accomplished, Arnau set off for the mainland and St. Augustine leaving the lighthouse keepers stranded on Cape Florida without a boat.[5]

In a matter of months the navy was on station off the Confederate coast. Although the vessels were not always in sight, the people on shore knew of the blockaders' presence. Two Confederate army deserters from St. Augustine, an Englishman and a Bostonian, stole a former United States Coast Survey sailboat and set out to join the Yankees. They successfully maneuvered their boat down the inland waterway to the Matanzas Inlet and then headed eastward. They were unconcerned about the perils of the sea for they were sure the blockaders would find them before any natural disasters overtook them. Comdr. S. W. Godon of the *Mohican* picked them up thirteen miles off shore near Brunswick, Georgia.[6]

Shortly after Flag Officer Samuel F. Du Pont captured Fernandina he sent his gunboats south to St. Augustine. On March 11, 1862, Comdr. C. R. P. Rodgers of the frigate *Wabash* anchored off the mouth of St. Augustine's harbor. The day before, Confederate soldiers, accompanied by a number of the town's civilians, had left for the interior. Mayor Christobal Bravo raised a white flag over Fort Marion,[7] whereupon, Commander Rodgers boarded a small boat and went to the town's wharf where he met the mayor in the midst of a crowd of curious onlookers. The two officials went to the town hall where the council was in session. Here Rodgers conducted the formal ceremony of surrender.[8]

---

5. Dorothy Dodd, ed., "Volunteers Report Destruction of Lighthouses," *Tequesta*, 19 (1954): 67-71; Moore, III, 23; Sec. of Treas. S. P. Chase to Sec. of Navy Gideon Welles, 11 October 1861, *Official Records of the Union and Confederate Navies in the War of the Rebellion* (Washington, GPO, 1894-1927), Series I, Volume 12, 216 (hereafter cited as ORN).
6. Comdr. S. W. Godon to Flag Officer S. F. Du Pont, 28 November 1861, ORN I: 12, 366.
7. When the United States acquired Florida the old Spanish fort, Castillo de San Marcos, was renamed Fort Marion.
8. Omega G. East, "St. Augustine During the Civil War," *Florida Historical Quarterly*, 31 (October 1952), 75-91.

Next Rodgers visited the clergy to assure them that the United States desired to have a peaceful, quiet occupation with as little disruption to daily life as possible. The ease of the take-over prompted Rodgers to report that "there are many citizens who are earnestly attached to the Union, a large number who are silently opposed to it, and a still larger number who care very little about the matter."[9]

It was from the distaff side that Rodgers found belligerent actions. The ladies had cut down the town's flagpole so that the Stars and Stripes could not be raised over St. Augustine. A Mrs. Mitchell marched up to him and declared that "the men had behaved like cowards, but there were stout hearts in other bosoms (striking her own)." Rodgers commented after the event that the women "seem to mistake treason for courage, and have a theatrical desire to figure as heroines."[10]

Rodgers recommended that the town hoist the Union flag and the mayor promptly ordered the Stars and Stripes flown from the flagstaff of Fort Marion. The Mayor wanted to turn over to Rodgers the five operational guns at the fort which had been left behind when the Confederate forces departed, but the commander declined, stating that he would hold the mayor responsible for the guns until Federal forces could occupy the town. Commander Rodgers had to remain in town overnight as the water over the bar became too choppy to allow him to return to the *Wabash*, which had too deep a draft to enter St. Augustine's harbor.[11]

A week later, on March 18, Lt. J. W. A. Nicholson, commanding officer of the *Isaac Smith*, entered St. Augustine harbor with a marine battalion commanded by Maj. Isaac T. Doughty, augmented by an army company of the Seventh New Hampshire Regiment. Nicholson's first act was to mount an 8-inch gun upon the ramparts of Fort Marion to command the main road into the city. Later, after army troops moved in to garrison St. Augustine, Major Doughty's marines loaded aboard ship for duty elsewhere. St. Augustine's new mayor, G. A. Pacetti, and the city council not only sent a letter commending the marines for their service to the town, but requested that the marines be returned, if it was compatible with the government's plan.[12]

Nicholson took possession of the post office property left behind by the fleeing postmaster. He also requested that a post office be established at St. Augustine similar to the one at Port Royal so that the people could communicate with relatives and friends in the north. He had forwarded some letters north, but there was no way that answers could be received without a post office in St. Augustine.[13]

9. Comdr. C. R. P. Rodgers to Du Pont, 12 March 1862, ORN I: 12, 595-97.

10. *Ibid.* Mrs. Mitchell is identified only as "the widow of a Doctor Loring, killed a few years ago at the St. Nicholas Hotel," 596, Du Pont to Comdr. P. Drayton, 14 March 1862, 601; East, 75-91.

11. Rodgers to Du Pont, 12 March 1862, ORN I: 12, 595-97.

12. G. A. Pacetti, Mayor, et. al. to Du Pont, 25 March 1862, *Ibid.*, 659-60.

13. Lt. J. W. A. Nicholson to Du Pont, 21 March 1862, *Ibid.*, 643-44.

People loyal to the United States told Lieutenant Nicholson of Paul Arnau's exploits in destroying the lighthouses along Florida's east coast. Nicholson brought Arnau aboard his ship and threatened to keep him under arrest if he did not produce the missing government lighthouse machinery. Arnau dispatched some carts to the countryside where he had hidden the Cape Canaveral and St. Augustine gear, all of it carefully packed and preserved. Nicholson released Arnau after he had his equipment. A year later Acting Master Henry A. Crane, a former resident of St. Augustine serving in the Union navy, found the Jupiter lighthouse equipment while on an expedition inland up the St. Lucie River.[14]

For the duration of the war St. Augustine remained in Union hands, serving as a rest camp for Federal forces. The United States made no major effort to extend its control over territory much beyond the city proper. An example of the safety and security of the town may be found in the reason for ordering the Seventh New Hampshire Regiment to St. Augustine. On February 13, 1862, it embarked in New York for Fort Jefferson, on Dry Tortugas in the Florida keys. En route a virulent form of smallpox broke out aboard ship. While at Fort Jefferson the regiment performed fatigue duty which included strenuous drilling and heavy artillery practice. Although the duty was not dangerous, it was severe and the muster roll for May showed 128 on the sick list and 25 absent with sick leave. During this period smallpox again swept through the troops. The regiment was transferred to Port Royal in June where typhoid fever raged among the soldiers. Finally, on September 1 the troops were sent to St. Augustine for light duty and rest.[15]

The blockade and Union troops closed St. Augustine's harbor, its front door, to all outside contacts except from Northern ships. In 1863 Noah Brooks, a Washington, D. C. based newspaper man for the Sacramento (California) *Daily Union*, noted that "the harbor is deserted, save when an occasional Government transport makes the echoes with its shrill steam whistle." He felt that the single regiment in garrison was sufficient to close the port to blockade-runners, and he commented that "these soldiers live in clover, having a delightful climate, a fine old town, plenty of fresh meat, fish, vegetables, fruit and milk."[16]

Early in 1864 Col. J. T. Otis, Tenth Connecticut Volunteers, reported he had 180 men fit for duty. His troops included 16 musicians, 30 men assigned to staff departments, and "50 recruits, who have never been initiated into the mysteries of handling a musket." He concluded

---

14. Acting Master H. A. Crane to Lt. Comdr. E. English, 4 March 1863, ORN I: 17, 372.
15. New Hampshire Legislature, *Revised Register of the Soldiers and Sailors of New Hampshire in the War of the Rebellion, 1861-1866* (Concord, Ira C. Evans, Public Printer, 1895), 350-51.
16. P. J. Staudenraus, ed., "A War Correspondent's View of St. Augustine and Fernandina: 1863," *Florida Historical Quarterly*, 41 (July 1962): 60-61.

that his command was "entirely inadequate to furnish a proper picket and provost guard in case of actual danger from outside."[17]

The question to be asked is why was St. Augustine so peaceful when protected by so few? Especially when these troops made no effort to extend their control beyond the town limits. The answer is to be found in the navy's riverine patrol of the St. Johns River—St. Augustine's back-door blockade. While Commander Rodgers was approaching St. Augustine on the Atlantic other naval units were entering the St. Johns River. These ships, based at Mayport Mills at the mouth of the river, made patrols as far upriver as Lake George. It was this back-door blockade which limited Confederate activity on the east bank of the St. Johns River to a few hit-and-run expeditions. The danger of being trapped on the wrong side of the river by Union gunboats demanded caution.

The Confederate reaction to the navy's patrols was to order all residents living on the banks of the river, who were suspected of disloyalty, to move inland ten miles. It also destroyed all small boats along the banks so that dissidents would not be able to communicate with the enemy forces afloat.[18]

After the gunboats entered the St. Johns River many Unionists sought safety with the blockaders. When the Union troops evacuated Jacksonville in April 1862, a group of loyalists who wanted to go to St. Augustine were transported there aboard the *Belvedere*. Two months later Comdr. Daniel Ammen, on patrol, picked up a Northern lady and a Confederate soldier who had deserted. A few weeks later Lieutenant Nicholson took aboard the Myers and Tombs families, 17 people. Both families fled to the navy because they had been ordered to move into the interior.[19]

The blockaders were also eliminating boats along the St. Johns. Comdr. Maxwell Woodhull reported destroying "perhaps a thousand boats. They were so numerous on our first appearance in the river it might almost be said to be 'bridged over.' " He was doing this to keep the Confederate regular and guerrilla forces from crossing to the eastern shore to bother Unionists. Of course, navy ships carried oared boats and the blockaders could communicate with individuals on shore at will.[20]

The destruction of small boats along the St. Johns River was detrimental to the Southerners because it destroyed their means of crossing the river. Later when the Confederates executed raids upon the east

---

17. Col. J. L. Otis to Brig. Gen. J. W. Turner, 22 February 1864, *War of the Rebellion: A Compilation of the Official Records of the Union and Confederate Armies* (Washington, GPO, 1880-1901), Series I, Volume 35, Part 1, 489 (hereafter cited as ORA).
18. Nicholson to Du Pont, 1-14, July 1862, ORN I: 13, 163-64.
19. Lt. Daniel Ammen to Du Pont, 11 June 1862, *Ibid.*, 90-91, Nicholson to Du Pont, 1-14 July 1862, 163-64; Richard A. Martin and Daniel L. Schafer, *Jacksonville's Ordeal By Fire* (Jacksonville, Florida Publishing Company, 1984), 218-24.
20. Comdr. Maxwell Woodhull to Comdr. Charles Steedman, 7 October 1862, ORN I: 13, 367, S. L. Burnett to Woodhull, 29 November 1862, ORN I: 13, 467.

Florida State Archives

Mayport Mills where the ships of the back-door blockade were based.

Confederate cavalry crossing the St. Johns River.

From *Dickison and his Men* by Mary Elizabeth Dickison.

bank, horses and wagons were ferried over on unwieldy rafts. Such awkward vessels, if caught in midstream, would be extremely vulnerable to the blockaders' gunboats.

On April 7, 1862, Gov. John Milton wrote to Pres. Jefferson Davis that the retirement of Confederate forces from Fernandina and the St. Johns River had demoralized many of the Florida troops and it had a serious impact upon the citizenry. He said that as soon as he could he would declare Florida east of the St. Johns to be under martial law because so many citizens had already demonstrated they were ready to submit to the enemy at the first opportunity.[21]

A few days later Gen. Richard F. Floyd, the Confederate commander of the state troops, received firsthand information on east Florida from Capt. J. W. Pearson of the Ochlawaha Rangers. "At least three-fourths of the people on the St. Johns River and east of it are aiding and abetting the enemy; we could see them at all times through the day communicating with the vessel in their small boats." He went on: "It is not safe for a small force to be on the east side of the river; there is great danger of being betrayed into the hands of the enemy."[22] He said he had two or three men already marked for hanging.

General Floyd wrote to Governor Milton on April 11 suggesting that the eastern counties be placed under martial law as they "contain a nest of traitors and lawless negroes." Just as soon as he had sufficient units he would move in, for "Thus far treason has boldly appeared in our midst with impunity; the hour to deal with it summarily has arrived."[23] Unfortunately for both the governor and the general, the military situation was not such that they could deal with it promptly or effectively.

A few days after Captain Pearson wrote to General Floyd he took his men to the east bank near Orange Mills to ambush a Union detachment expected to arrive momentarily. On the Friday night of April 11 Pearson made his crossing to secure secrecy. By dawn some of his men were still on the west bank. Pearson remained in hiding until dark when the rest of his men could join him. But just at dusk a gunboat hove in sight and anchored about four miles below the mills. The captain decided that it was useless to attempt a surprise attack with only a portion of his men and in the face of a Union gunboat. He remained hidden until the next night when he recrossed the river. By early Monday morning Pearson and his men were seven miles inland from Palatka heading back to camp.

F. L. Dancy, who had brought Pearson the information of the Union troops' move to Orange Mills, stated: "I am convinced [the ambush] failed through information furnished them by traitors living in our midst and communicating with the enemy with impunity by means of boats

21. Gov. John Milton to Pres. Jefferson Davis, 7 April 1862, ORA I: 6, 426-27.
22. Capt. J. W. Pearson to Brig. Gen. R. F. Floyd, 8 April 1862, ORA I: 53, 233-34.
23. Floyd to Milton, 11 April 1862, *Ibid.*, 232-33.

and otherwise. There were not less than four boats from different points on the river that communicated with the propeller [the gunboat] during Sunday."[24]

In addition to white Unionists the Southern blacks became important to the navy. Slavery was one of the central issues of the Civil War, yet the problem of what to do with the Negro once he joined, or was liberated by, the Union forces was not immediately solved. President Lincoln, in his desire to hold the border states within the Union repeatedly stated that the war was to preserve the United States. He steadfastly refused to include the slave in his war aims. Congress was of the same mind when, the day after the First Battle of Bull Run, it passed resolutions disclaiming any intention to alter the states' established institutions. Until the government included the elimination of slavery within its wartime aims, the status of the escaped slave was a thorny problem confronting military and naval officers in the war zones.

What did one do with Southern slaves? Gen. Benjamin F. Butler faced the question early in the conflict when a Confederate officer came to him to claim some runaway Negroes. Butler used the subtle language of international law and called them "contraband of war." He refused to turn them over. This term, a phrase immediately adopted in most military communications, allowed the slave to be kept without unduly disturbing the slave-owning population of the border states aligned with the North.[25] Later, indiscriminate use of the term by naval officers found it referring to any black man from the South within Northern lines.

Early in the war Secretary of the Navy Gideon Welles had to face the problem of what to do with Southern blacks who fled to navy ships. He decided that, although it was not the official policy to encourage the desertions of such persons, they would be allowed to remain on board as a principle of humanity.[26] By September 1861 Welles determined that contrabands could not be sent back to the control of the Confederacy, yet they could not remain idle drawing navy rations, nor was it proper to compel them to work without compensation; therefore, he authorized their enlistment "under the same form and regulations as apply to other enlistments."[27] However, he stipulated that contrabands could not be enlisted at a rating higher than boys (an apprentice rating in the navy), which entitled them to $10.00 per month and one ration per day.

Thus early in the war the navy enlisted blacks under the same rules as whites, a practice the army never did adopt. When the army finally enlisted blacks it was in separate units. The practice of both services followed earlier regulations. Congress had specifically excluded black

24. Col. F. L. Dancy to Floyd, 12 April 1862, *Ibid.*, 234-36.
25. Willie Lee Rose, *Rehearsal for Reconstruction* (New York, Vintage Books, 1967), 13-14.
26. Gideon Welles to Flag Officer Silas H. Stringham, 22 July 1861, reprinted in Boynton, 2: 28; Flag Officer Wm. Mervine to Welles, 11 July 1861, ORN I: 16, 580.
27. Welles to Flag Officer W. M. McKean, 25 September 1861, ORN I: 16, 689.

men from service in the army, but it did not impose these restrictions upon the navy. The navy always had black sailors serving side by side with whites. In fact, the calling of the sea, both in the merchant fleet and the navy, had been one of the limited opportunities available to free Negroes in pre-war days.[28]

By July 1862 Secretary Welles instructed the East Gulf Blockading Squadron to ship (enlist) on board as many contrabands as possible because Northern enlistments had not kept pace with the needs of the navy.[29] Later Welles issued instructions that no contrabands could be accepted into the navy with a higher rating than landsman, but they could become, if qualified, coal heavers, firemen, ordinary seamen, or seamen; however, they could not be transferred to another ship except as landsmen.[30] Welles's new policy allowed the navy to increase the number of blacks in service.

Often the contraband provided valuable services as a pilot or guide. The escaped slave's position was especially dangerous on those expeditions into the interior because the enemy showed little mercy towards a captured contraband. The black pilot aboard the *Penguin* is a case in point. In late March 1862 Federal authorities received word that a blockade-runner had brought an arms shipment into Mosquito Inlet. Lt. Thomas A. Budd organized an expedition of five or six boats to search for the arms. Budd took the inland passage and proceeded 15 to 18 miles south of New Smyrna before giving up. On his return his boats were ambushed by Confederates hidden on shore in the dense underbrush. The heavy fire pouring in from the cover killed Budd, another officer, and two sailors instantly. Two others were seriously injured and the black pilot had a slight wound in his foot. All sailors in Budd's boat were captured. The Negro pilot was summarily hanged.[31]

The small coastal steamer *Darlington*, one of the prizes taken when the navy captured Fernandina, became an army transport. The navy provided a contraband crew familiar with the local waters. Comdr. Percival Drayton, a native South Carolinian, left instructions for his relief

28. Long before the war some Southern states had enacted legislation barring free blacks from moving into the state, and they used these statutes to keep black merchant sailors aboard ship while their vessels were in port. When Florida was a territory, it too had laws forbidding the migration of free Negroes into its territory. During the Second Seminole War Lt. John T. McLaughlin, commanding the schooner *Flirt*, had trouble when the sheriff in Key West arrested some of his colored sailors under this act, McLaughlin to secretary of the navy, 10 July 1840, RG 45, Letters Received by the secretary of the navy from officers below the rank of commander ("Officers Letters"), 1802-1889, National Archives, Washington, D. C.; George E. Buker, *Swamp Sailors: Riverine Warfare in the Everglades, 1835-1842* (Gainesville, University Presses of Florida, 1975), 108-09.

29. Welles to Flag Officers J. L. Lardner and D. G. Farragut, 2 July 1862, ORN I: 17, 269.

30. Landsman was a rating for a person who had no knowledge of seamanship, Hamersly, 422; Harold D. Langley, *Social Reform in the United States Navy, 1798-1862* (Urbana, University of Illinois Press, 1967), 95.

31. Albert Warren Kelsey, *Autobiographical Notes and Memoranda on the Blockade, 1861 to 1863* (Baltimore, Munder-Thomsen Press, 1911), 44-46; *Florida Sentinel* (Tallahassee), 1 April 1862; Du Pont to Welles, 24 March 1862, ORN I: 12, 645-51.

Florida State Archives.

Prince, contraband pilot of the *Uncas*.

concerning the precautions he employed on the *Darlington* because of her contraband crew. Normally when she went out on an expedition beyond local waters he put an officer, engineer, and 10 to 40 armed men aboard to protect the crew.[32]

In their dispatches, some commanding officers singled out contrabands for their deeds. Isaac Tattnall had been a pilot on the *St. Marys*, plying between Wassaw Sound, Georgia, and St. Marys River. He brought valuable knowledge of Georgia and northeast Florida waters to the blockaders. Lieutenant Nicholson borrowed Prince, the contraband pilot of the *Uncas*, to take his ship which had a draft of 10′ 8″, up the St. Johns River. Nicholson said that without Prince's aid he would have had to move cautiously. Acting Masters Mate John C. Champion singled out Henry, ship's cook of the *Columbine*, and Willie, cook of the *Sumter*, for their parts in the *Columbine*'s capture of two Confederate steamers, the *Hattie* and the *Sumter*.[33]

Drover Edwards, a landsman aboard the *Columbine* when she was captured by Capt. J. J. Dickison of the Second Florida Cavalry, demonstrated the security of the east bank of the St. Johns. In May 1864 the *Columbine* had gone up to Volusia to check on the safety of the army detachments along the river. On her return, her captain, expecting to be fired upon by rebel infantry at Horse Landing, called all hands to quarters. During his approach he began shelling the shore. Dickison, concealed on the west bank, waited until the ship was no more than thirty yards distant before opening fire. The *Columbine*'s forward gun and wheel ropes were hit. Before the steering mechanism could be restored, she went aground to lay at the mercy of the enemy. The skirmish lasted less than an hour. During that time both guns were put out of commission and the carnage on deck caused Ens. Frank Sanborn to strike his colors. Because no contraband could look forward to good treatment upon being captured, many of the colored troops and seamen jumped in the river to try for the east bank, Edwards among them. He saw four black soldiers and a contraband shipmate, William Moran, sink below the waters. Later he came across three soldiers of the Thirty-fifth United States Colored Troops, and the four unarmed men made their way safely to St. Augustine, after a five-day trip through the wilderness.[34]

The eastern shore of the St. Johns River was a safe haven for Northerners and their supporters. Here Confederate scouts seldom operated. Southern Maj. Gen. Patton Anderson, commanding the District of Florida, acknowledged his inability to observe Union movements on the east

32. Comdr. P. Drayton to Lt. Comdr. A. G. Clary, 16 May 1862, ORN I: 13, 43.
33. *Ibid.*, Nicholson to Rodgers, 17 June 1862, 109; Acting Master J. C. Champion to Comdr. G. C. Balch, 23 March 1864, ORN I: 15, 300-03.
34. *Ibid.*, Balch to R. Adm. J. A. Dahlgren, 12 June 1864, 448-49; Ens. Frank Sanborn to Dahlgren, 3 September 1864, 451-53; Mary Elizabeth Dickison, *Dickison and His Men: Reminiscences of the War in Florida*, ed. Samuel Proctor (Gainesville, University of Florida Press, 1962), 65-67.

From *Dickison and his Men.*

Capture of the gunboat *Columbine*.

bank. When the enemy withdrew four regiments from Palatka and carried them across to Picolata, Anderson did not know if they had marched to St. Augustine to be shipped North or marched down the east bank to Jacksonville. He commented that the parallelogram bounded by St. Augustine, Picolata, Jacksonville and the mouth of the St. Johns River was "wholly within the enemy's possession and . . . it was impossible to keep ourselves well advised of all his movements on that side of the river."[35]

Official dispatches from both sides attest to the effectiveness of St. Augustine's back-door blockade. Finally in March 1864 the Confederates mined the 25-foot channel off Mandarin Point. If this channel could be blocked it would free the upper St. Johns of Union gunboats and army transports. During April and May the Union lost three ships, and for a month river activity was curtailed until the remaining torpedoes (mines in present-day terminology) were removed.[36] This was the last effective challenge to the navy on the St. Johns.

Begining in 1863 and continuing throughout the war the Unionist refugee flow to St. Augustine increased as disillusioned, war-weary civilians and Confederate deserters joined the trek. William Burr Jones, a native of Connecticut who had moved to Orange Springs for his health, was conscripted, but poor health kept him from serving. He asked to go to St. Augustine. It was October 1864 before he was able to take his family through the lines. He had received no news from his parents in Connecticut since November 1860. Once in St. Augustine he was among friends for a Connecticut regiment garrisoned the town.

The following February, Jones wrote home that some of the troops acted imprudently when they went ten miles out of town unarmed to attend a dance, for all were captured by a Confederate raiding party.[37] The dancers had been captured by Captain Dickison during an extended sweep into the east bank of the St. Johns.

Another incident of that same sweep provides an astonishing glimpse of the loyalists east of the back-door blockade. Dickison learned that Lt. Col. Albert H. Wilcoxon of the Seventeenth Connecticut was headed down the Old Government Road toward Volusia county. At the next dwelling he and ten men, all dressed in blue overcoats taken from the Union soldiers captured at the dance, left the main body of troops to approach the farm house. The woman there thought they were Union soldiers and professed her loyalty to the North. She even confided that two of her sons had deserted from the Confederate army and were at that moment hiding in a nearby swamp because they had nearly been

35. Maj. Gen. Patton Anderson to Capt. H. W. Feilden, 14 May 1864, ORA I: 35, Part 1, 371.

36. Balch to Cmdr. S. C. Rowan, 1 April 1864, ORN I: 15, 307: U. S. Coast Survey Asst. C. O. Boutelle to U. S. Coast Survey Supt. A. D. Bache, 11 May 1864, 426-28; Arch Fredric Blakey, *Parade of Memories* (Jacksonville, Clay County Bicentennial Steering Committee, 1976), 83; Martin, 218-24.

37. William Burr Jones to Russell Jones, 16 October 1864, 9 February 1865, MC 16, St. Augustine Historical Society Library; Dickison, 115-17.

From *Dickison and his Men.*

Capt. J. J. Dickison, C. S. A.

From *Dickison and his Men.*

Confederate cavalry recrossing the St. Johns with prisoners, captured wagons and stores.

captured by Dickison just two nights earlier. She said that they would remain in hiding until they heard that Dickison had recrossed the river.

While this conversation was going on some of Dickison's men, not dressed in blue overcoats, rode up, dismounted, and began watering their horses. Captain Dickison quickly called her attention to the rebels he "had captured from Dickison's raiders." At the same time he gave orders to his blue-coated men to guard his "prisoners" well.

Captain Dickison promised to pay the woman for the fodder his men used, but then he remembered he had only Confederate money to offer her and it had no value on that side of the river. He finally said that on his return his quartermaster would provide her with the equivalent value in coffee and flour. When he prepared to leave the woman hugged him and begged him to capture that rebel Dickison.[38]

Dickison continued to follow Wilcoxon's trail. Every few miles he met deserters on their way to St. Augustine. Riding at the head of his blue-coated troops, he would call these people rebels. They denied his charge, declaring to be good Union men who had deserted from the Confederate army. After quizzing the men concerning Colonel Wilcoxon, Dickison would send them to the rear as prisoners. Ultimately this raid netted him Colonel Wilcoxon's entire command: 75 soldiers, 10 wagons loaded with Sea Island cotton, and some of the Union's finest cavalry horses.[39]

Two quotes from contemporary sources clearly demonstrate the success of St. Augustine's back-door blockade. In May 1864 John C. Gray, Jr., a Federal officer, stated that "the people on the east side of the St. Johns are called Florida Yankees and the majority of them are Union men."[40] Two months later Lake City's *Columbian* voiced the same sentiments in an editorial praising Captain Dickison while wishing that he had a larger command so that: "We would soon hear of the evacuation of Lincoln's congressional district in East Florida."[41] The Union blockade, especially the back-door blockade on the St. Johns River, had a significant impact upon St. Augustine during the Civil War.

38. Dickison, 118-19.
39. *Ibid.*, 119-24.
40. John F. Reiger, "Florida After Secession: Abandonment By the Confederacy and Its Consequences," *Florida Historical Quarterly*, 50 (October 1971), 139.
41. Dickison, 73.

The Home Front: Civil War Times in St. Augustine

Thomas Graham

For fourteen months following secession St. Augustine was a part of the Confederacy, but for the remaining three years of the Civil War the town was occupied by the military forces of the United States. During the time that St. Augustine was under Confederate control an attempt was made to revolutionize the political and economic institutions of the community, as well as to build a spirit of Southern nationalism. Then, following United States occupation, Federal forces endeavored to restore St. Augustine to the Union. As a result the community experienced four years of internal strife and turmoil, even though the battles of the war were fought far from the town.

While the spirit of Southern nationalism had existed for a long time before secession, the impulse toward Southern independence and the attempt to create a Southern nation began in the fall of 1859. The revolutionary abolitionist John Brown sent the South into action with his abortive attempt to incite a slave rebellion at Harper's Ferry, Virginia. In St. Augustine the local newspaper, Matthias Andreu's *Examiner*, warned that any further violent action by Northern "fanatics" would plunge the country into "all the horrors of civil war."[1] Although tempers subsided after a few weeks, an undercurrent of distrust continued to run strongly in the South. The *Examiner* adopted a new motto: "Equality in the Union and Nothing Less."

When it became evident in the fall of the next year that Abraham Lincoln, a sectional candidate who drew support and votes only in the North, would be elected president, radical secessionists in the slave states demanded that the Southern people take themselves out of the Union. Andreu's editorials in the *Examiner* had at first held out hope of reconciliation with the North, but Lincoln's election committed him to a policy of immediate secession. Andreu argued that the South had no choice: the North was dominated by violent abolitionists who intended to unleash the South's slaves on a rampage of murder and rape. Only by secession and formation of its own government could the South protect itself.[2]

The results of the 1860 election in St. Johns County seem to indicate that the people in the area agreed with Andreu. The Unionist candidates

---

Thomas Graham is professor of history at Flagler College, St. Augustine, Florida. He is the author of *The Awakening of St. Augustine.*

1. *St. Augustine Examiner*, 12 November 1859.
2. *Ibid.*, 29 December 1860.

for governor and president were soundly defeated by the regular Democratic candidates, who were popularly regarded as the pro-secession candidates. No votes for Lincoln were recorded in the county, nor, indeed, in the entire state.[3]

Events moved rapidly after the election. "Secession flags" blossomed from the balconies of houses and town citizens pinned "secession cockades" to their lapels.[4] On December 15 a secession convention assembled in the court house to nominate delegates to the state secession convention. Matthew Solana and R. G. Mays, both of whom favored immediate secession, were unanimously nominated by the 21 men in attendance. In the following week's election Solana and Mays were chosen without opposition. The *Examiner* expressed disappointment that few St. Augustinians turned out to vote, but interpreted this as a sign of unanimous support for secession, rather than opposition or indifference. So far as the *Examiner* was concerned, the only division among local people was between those who favored immediate secession and those who wanted to postpone secession.[5]

In Tallahassee on January 10, 1861, St. Augustine's delegates voted with the majority in favor of the ordinance of secession. When news arrived in St. Augustine, the town celebrated independence with the pealing of church bells, musket volleys, ceremonial flag raisings, and, in the evening, bonfires and a torchlight parade.[6]

One of St. Augustine's leading residents, George R. Fairbanks, a pioneer chronicler of Florida's history, traveled to Tallahassee to address the convention of the new government. His speech put secession in historical context. Fairbanks pointed out that during its history Florida had experienced six changes in government, and he emphasized that its connection with the United States had been brief: "twenty-four years of territorial vassalage" followed by only sixteen years of statehood. Now Florida had justifiably asserted its independence to protect her "rights and interests."[7]

The people of St. Augustine were caught up in the emotional tide of Southern patriotism. Ceremonial occasions provided an opportunity to build Southern national consciousness and solidarity. Washington's Birthday witnessed a parade by the local militia units, the St. Augustine Blues and the Governor's Guards. Orators praised Washington as a great Southern revolutionary leader and defender of independence. News of the fall of Fort Sumter set off another round of public celebra-

3. Tallahassee *Floridian and Journal*, 17 November 1860.
4. *St. Augustine Examiner*, 8 December 1860.
5. *Ibid.*, 14, 22, 29 December 1860.
6. *Ibid.*, 19 January 1861; Ralph A. Wooster, "The Florida Secession Convention," *Florida Historical Quarterly* 26 (April 1958): 385.
7. George R. Fairbanks, Address to the State Convention, 21 April 1861, typed copy, Biographical File, Buckingham Smith, St. Augustine Historical Society Library (hereafter cited as Society Library).

tion. On the plaza a towering new flagpole proudly flew the new flag of the rebellion.[8]

Miss Anna Dummett, sister-in-law of Confederate General William Hardee, composed two heroic songs in honor of Florida's struggle for independence. Sung to the tune of "Maryland, My Maryland," the first verse of one ran: "Thy sons are able brave and strong/ They only wait to meet the foe/ Their dauntless bravery to show/ and lay the proud oppressor low."[9]

Leaders of the Catholic church professed to see a religious revival in St. Augustine. They declared that the fasts and abstinences of the Lenten season had been more carefully and fervently observed than in the less trying years before secession.[10]

The Catholic church in St. Augustine was unusual in that its spiritual leader, French-born Bishop Augustin Verot, was an open and avowed slavery advocate and secessionist. His influence may have been considerable in building Confederate loyalty among the large Minorcan population. Elsewhere in the South foreign-born individuals and distinct ethnic groups were more likely than the general population to hold Unionist sympathies, but St. Augustine's Minorcans seem to have sided overwhelmingly with the rebels.[11]

In St. Augustine, as in the rest of Florida, the secessionists had seized the initiative and had attracted the majority of the populace to their side. However, since it was clear that their attempt to create a Southern nation did not have the support of all the people, they moved to eliminate or silence the opposition. Shortly after the election of Lincoln a meeting of secessionists in St. Augustine passed a resolution urging all local residents to unite against "Black Republicans," demanding the expulsion "by force of arms" of anyone who attempted to speak out in favor of Northern ideas. The *Examiner* ran an emotional editorial avowing that the North was the enemy and that those who spoke in favor of the Union should desist. It declared, "the day is possibly not distant, when such talk will be punished as treason, and it is not improbable, some one of them may adorn a gallows."[12]

Citizens were warned to be alert for supposed abolitionist agitators who, it was feared, had infiltrated the South to "demoralize" the slaves. Some men took it upon themselves to form a vigilance committee to keep their eyes on "suspicious characters" in the community.[13] The handful of winter visitors who arrived in St. Augustine from the North were

---

8. *St. Augustine Examiner*, 2 March, 20 April 1861; Joseph H. Parks, *General Edmund Kirby Smith, C. S. A.* (Baton Rouge, L. S. U. Press, 1954), 112.
9. Song manuscripts, Biographical File, Dummett, Society Library.
10. Baltimore *Catholic Mirror*, 4 May 1861, Diocese of Florida Archives, Catholic Center, Mandarin.
11. Michael V. Gannon, *Rebel Bishop: The Life and Era of Augustin Verot* (Milwaukee, Bruce Publishing Co., 1964), 170-71.
12. *St. Augustine Examiner*, 24 November 1860.
13. *Ibid.*, 27 October, 1 December 1860.

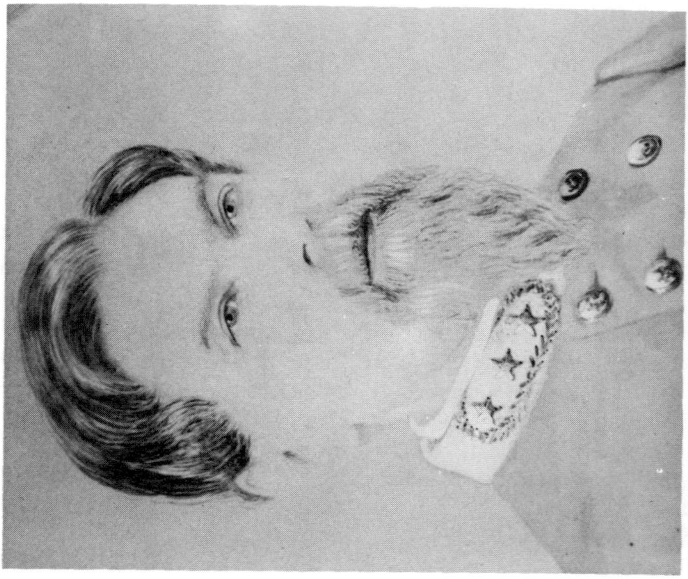

St. Augustine Historical Society.

Gen. William Hardee, C. S. A.

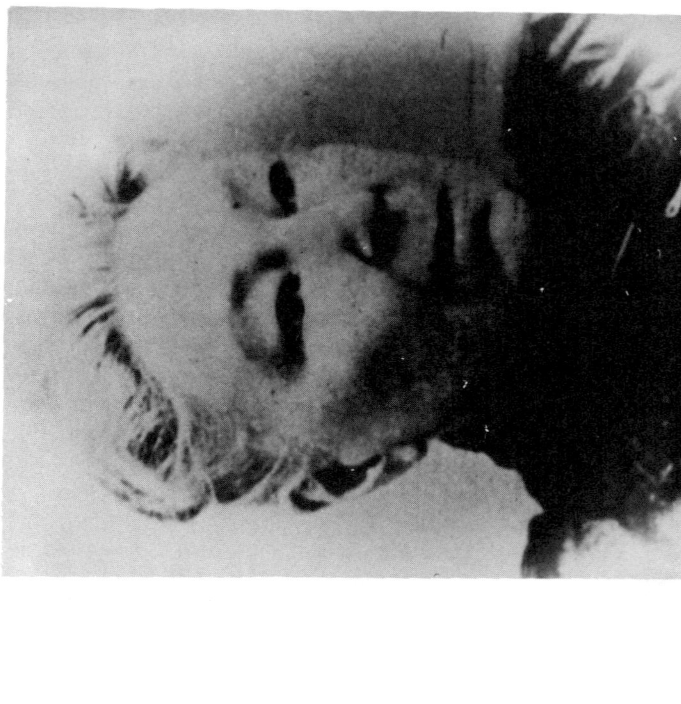

St. Augustine Historical Society.

Miss Anna Dummett, sister-in-law of William Hardee and composer of patriotic Confederate songs.

warned to keep their opinions to themselves if they wished to remain unmolested in town. Some natives went so far as to warn that all Northern "strangers," whether they be tourists or businessmen, should be considered enemies.[14]

It was proposed that all men over the age of 16 be required to swear an oath of allegiance to the Confederate States of America. This plan for a universal loyalty oath was not adopted by the state government and evidently was not carried out in St. Augustine.[15]

For most Floridians the act of secession settled the question of their loyalty. Some Unionists left for the North, but most of those who had doubted the wisdom of independence or who wanted to remain loyal to the United States acquiesced and accepted the new government.[16] In August 1861, the state government passed a law which permitted the confiscation of the property of "enemy aliens." This effectively intimidated those remaining few who stayed staunchly Unionist. Those loyal to the United States kept silent and were usually left alone, even when their Union sympathies were known or suspected.[17]

Having gained political independence, it remained to be seen if Florida could establish economic independence. The St. Augustine *Examiner* had been arguing for more than a year that the South would be more prosperous out of the Union than in. However, reality proved more harsh than rosy theory. Even before secession the money system began to break down as local merchants and banks refused to accept drafts and other paper drawn on Northern banks or even on out-of-state banks. By the summer of 1861 the city council was debating a proposal to print small denomination bills so that the town would at least have a medium of exchange for daily business.[18]

Just two months after Lincoln's election, Benjamin Wright penned this description of St. Augustine's economic situation:

> These "secession" movements have made quite a revolution in & about this "*ancient City*". Once it was the resort of many invalids & strangers, but is now wholly deserted by them. Those who reside here are in verry straightened circumstances & live "from hand to mouth." Provisions are verry scarce & dear & those who are not *too poor* to move seem determined to leave. Without giving

14. *Ibid.*, 9 March, 11 May, 22 June 1861.
15. *Ibid.*, 4 May, 22 June 1861; John E. Johns, *Florida During the Civil War* (Gainesville, University of Florida Press, 1963), 157.
16. Johns, 22.
17. *Ibid.*, 154.
18. City Council Minutes, 3 August 1861, St. Augustine City Papers, Society Library; *St. Augustine Examiner*, 3 March 1860; Clarissa C. Anderson to Andrew Anderson, 25 November 1859, Anderson Papers, MC 10, Society Library.

further details I can only say that "St. Augustine" is far from a desirable place to live in. . . .[19]

The *Examiner* put a brave face on the situation, declaring that the town could become a summer resort for Southerners rather than a winter resort for Yankees.[20] It praised the local citizens for growing their own food, observing that around town "each and every little spot has been put into cultivation." As long as the people could grow corn and potatoes and catch fish from the bay, the Union naval blockade which stopped commercial shipping by the end of 1861 would not starve the town into submission. Nevertheless, by summer the newspaper was running appeals for donations to a fund which would purchase food for the destitute. Significantly the *Examiner* published its appeal in an edition reduced to one-quarter its usual size because it was temporarily short of newsprint.[21]

All during the first year of secession St. Augustine's harbor was visited by occasional blockade-running vessels which brought in food and other supplies. However, these visits seem to have been infrequent. The most sensational episode to occur during this period was the wreck of the Confederate privateer *Jefferson Davis* on the sandbar at the harbor entrance in August, 1861.[22]

St. Augustine had been preparing to assert its independence with military force in obedience to Gov. Madison Starke Perry's call for reorganization of the state militia shortly after the John Brown raid. The city raised a local unit, organized in the spring of 1860, calling itself the Florida Independent Blues, often referred to as the St. Augustine Blues.[23] The Blues were joined by the Milton Guards in November 1860, and by the Marion Artillery in January 1861. The Guards was recruited from the younger boys of the town, while the Artillery was responsible for manning the cannon in the water battery along the seawall outside Fort Marion.[24] The fort had been seized on January 7, 1861, several days before secession. The lone United States Army sergeant in charge of the fort delivered the keys of the fort to the Confederates, offering only verbal resistance and asking only for a receipt.[25] Some of the cannon in

19. Benjamin Wright to George R. Fairbanks, 22 January 1861, copy, Fairbanks Papers, P. K. Yonge Library of Florida History, University of Florida, Gainesville.
20. *St. Augustine Examiner*, 15 June 1861.
21. *Ibid.*, 18 May, 8 June 1861.
22. Hannah Jenckes to Mary Martha Reid, 7 January 1862, Biographical File, Reid, Society Library; John H. Van Gorden, "Captain Coxetter and the *Jefferson Davis*," *El Escribano* 43 (April 1962): 4.
23. Johns, 5-7; *St. Augustine Examiner*, 19 May 1860.
24. *St. Augustine Examiner*, 1 December 1860; 26 January 1861.
25. Ord. Sgt. Henry Douglas to Col. H. K. Craig, 7 January 1861, *The War of the Rebellion: A Compilation of the Official Records of the Union and Confederate Armies* (Washington, GPO, 1880-1901), Series I, Volume 1, 333 (hereafter cited as ORA).

Fort Marion were immediately removed and sent to Fernandina and other points around the state.[26]

The willingness of Florida's soldiers to leave home and fight for the Confederacy on the front lines in Tennessee and Virginia was tested early. By the summer of 1861 the Confederate government had decided that attempting to defend Florida's coast was a hopeless task and that Florida's manpower could be put to better use elsewhere. Gen. Robert E. Lee inspected the coastal defenses as far south as Fernandina in November 1861 and declared that only the major ports of Charleston, Savannah, and Brunswick should be defended. He later added: "The small force posted at Saint Augustine serves only as an invitation to attack."[27]

When, in February 1862, Gen. U. S. Grant's forces captured two major Confederate forts in Tennessee and threatened an invasion of the South's heartland, the Confederacy was forced to order Florida's troops north into the breach. The state's new governor, John Milton, spoke for Florida's citizens when he declared that they had "almost despaired of protection from the Confederate Government."[28] He spoke the truth. The state was open to invasion and its people were demoralized.

Local government in St. Augustine was on the verge of collapse. At first secession had caused few changes in local politics. The town council had continued to concern itself with sanitation, streets, licenses, and the usual fare which had routinely come before it in previous years. However, by the fall of 1861 the council faced a crisis when it became apparent that many citizens would be hard pressed to pay their taxes. The town's economy had slowed to a standstill. Many of the town's men were away at war, the Northern tourists no longer filled the hotels, and the Union blockade of the seacoast had strangled trade.

Samuel Buffington, a prominent hotel operator, petitioned for a suspension of tax collections, but the council said that there was no other way to finance town government. At first the council threatened to prosecute those who were delinquent in their tax payments; then the town fathers agreed to postpone the tax collection deadline. Finally, early in 1862 the council began to cut out even the most basic government services. The town scavenger was suspended and the town's paupers were cut off from support.[29] Only the arrival of the Federal invasion force in March resolved the crisis and provided a radical resolution of the town government's dilemma. The secessionists' attempt to create a Southern nation had, in St. Augustine, come to an inglorious end.

26. J. Gardner, "Removal of Guns, Arms and Munitions From Fort Marion, at St. Augustine, Florida, January 6th–12th, 1861," Miscellaneous File, St. Augustine History, Civil War Period, Society Library.

27. Gen. R. E. Lee to Gen. S. Cooper, 21 November 1861, ORA I: 6, 327; Lee to Gen. J. H. Trapier, 13 March 1862, ORA I: 6, 406.

28. John F. Reiger, "Florida After Secession: Abandonment by the Confederacy and Its Consequences," *Florida Historical Quarterly* 50 (October 1971): 129-131.

29. City Council Minutes, 26 September, 14 December 1861; 6 January, 3 March 1862.

The United States had not been in a hurry to conquer Florida, even though it was only lightly defended, because there was little strategic value to occupying the peninsula's sand and swamps. Gen. George McClellan stated the North's priorities when he declared that Charleston should be the major objective on the South Atlantic coast, but he added, "Saint Augustine might as well be taken by way of an interlude. . . ."[30]

One person who was quite anxious to see St. Augustine in Federal hands was Buckingham Smith, a Unionist exile from the Ancient City living in New York City. In February 1862, the Confederate government had begun proceedings under its alien properties act to confiscate Smith's property. Somehow Smith had learned of this threat and had written Secretary of State William H. Seward asking why the Federal government had not reoccupied St. Augustine since the rebels were not attempting to defend Florida. It is doubtful that Smith's letter had any great impact on United States policy, but its logic shortly became the basis of military action.[31]

On February 28 a fleet of 26 United States Navy ships set sail from Department of the South headquarters at Hilton Head, South Carolina, to occupy Fernandina, Jacksonville, and St. Augustine. On March 8 the first scout ship arrived off the St. Augustine inlet and dropped bouys in the channel to mark the entrance for the following ships. Four days later in a small boat flying a white flag of truce Comdr. C. R. P. Rodgers left Flag Officer Samuel Du Pont's flagship *Wabash* to receive the surrender of St. Augustine.[32]

Du Pont had earlier been told by Union sympathizers that the troops at St. Augustine would not resist and that the populace was disillusioned with the war. Du Pont also expected to find a large number of Unionists in St. Augustine because the town had had such a close contact with the North through tourism and immigration before the war. Du Pont felt that "if there were any people on this coast likely to remain in their houses it would be at St. Augustine."[33]

Commander Rogers was met at the seawall by Mayor Cristobal Bravo, other members of the town council, and a few Unionists. Rogers informed the municipal leaders that the Federal authorities "had a single purpose—to restore the state of affairs which existed before the rebellion."[34] He assured the councilmen that local government would continue

30. Maj. Gen. George B. McClellan to Gen. Thomas W. Sherman, 14 February 1862, ORA I: 6, 225.

31. Summons, Confederate States of America, District of Florida, Eastern Division to Elizabeth Gardner, typed copy, Biographical File, Buckingham Smith, Society Library; Buckingham Smith to William H. Seward, 26 February 1862, *Official Records of the Union and Confederate Navies in the War of the Rebellion* (Washington, GPO, 1894-1927), Series I, Volume 12, 622-23 (hereafter cited as ORN).

32. Johns, 62; Flag Officer Samuel Du Pont to Comdr. W. E. LeRoy, 8 March 1862, ORN I; 12, 588; LeRoy to Du Pont, 10 March 1862, ORN I: 12, 592-93; Du Pont to Gideon Welles, 13 March 1862, ORN I: 12, 599.

33. Du Pont to Welles, 9 March 1862, ORN I: 12, 588-89; Du Pont to Welles, 13 March 1862, ORN I: 12, 599; Brig. Gen. H. G. Wright to Du Pont, 5 March 1862, ORN I: 12, 581-82.

34. Comdr. C. R. P. Rodgers to Du Pont, 12 March 1862, ORN I: 12, 595.

to administer affairs in town. At his suggestion the party walked to Fort Marion where the town leaders raised the Stars and Stripes. At the conclusion of these actions marking the beginning of reconstruction in St. Augustine, Du Pont wrote to Secretary of the Navy Gideon Welles: "The American flag is flying once more over that old city, raised by the hands of its own people, who resisted the appeals, threats, and falsehoods of their leaders, though compelled to witness the carrying off of their sons in the ranks of the flying enemy."[35]

At first it appeared things might work out smoothly. The Federals moved to establish a post office so that regular communication with the North could be resumed, and a supply of small denomination United States currency was requested since St. Augustine was devoid of a medium of exchange, "except for the wretched paper currency of the rebellion."[36] The town council voted to place guards at the fort and St. Francis Barracks. A municipal election was even held, and G. A. Pacetti sworn in as the new mayor. An indication of social change can be seen in the council's decision to pay the city marshal a salary and suspend the fees which the marshal formerly received for "punishing negroes." (The secretary recording the minutes had at first started to write "whipping negroes," but had crossed it out.)[37]

Although the Federals were optimistic about the Union loyalties of the town's citizenry, there had been no doubt from the start that some of the natives were staunch rebel sympathizers. During his first walk around the streets Commander Rogers had met with dramatic vocal opposition from several women. Other ladies chopped down the flagpole which had been erected on the plaza to celebrate secession so that no American flag would ever fly upon it. Hannah Jenckes expressed the feelings of many St. Augustine women when she called the men who were willing to cooperate with the Federals "a set of Granies."[38] It soon became apparent to the occupying forces that they had overestimated Unionist sympathies in the town.

The Federals may have also underestimated the military threat which the Confederates would be able to mount against the invasion. At first the town was occupied only by a small force of marines from the Navy's fleet and one company from the Fourth New Hampshire Volunteers under the command of Col. Louis Bell. When the marines were withdrawn, Colonel Bell became alarmed and asked for reinforcements. Since none could be sent, he was ordered to keep his troops in and around the fort and let the townspeople fend for themselves. The

35. *Ibid.*, 595-97; Du Pont to Welles, 13 March 1862, ORN I: 12, 599; Lt. J. W. A. Nicholson to Du Pont, 21 March 1862, ORN I: 12, 644.

36. Rodgers to Du Pont, 12 March 1862, ORN I: 12, 595; Nicholson to Du Pont, 21 March 1862, ORN I: 12, 643-44.

37. City Council Minutes, 22, 24 March 1862.

38. Jenckes to Reid, 10 March 1862; Du Pont to Comdr. Percival Drayton, 14 March 1862, ORN I: 12, 601-02.

National Archives.

United States Post Headquarters, December 10, 1864, seen from King Street looking south on St. George Street. The Trinity Episcopal Church parish hall now occupies the site.

commanding general on the scene, Brig. Gen. H. G. Wright, felt this would do as a temporary expedient since it appeared most of the townspeople were rebel sympathizers and therefore not needing or deserving Federal protection.[39]

However, those natives who had openly revealed their Unionism and welcomed the invaders were dismayed at the prospect that they might now be abandoned to the revenge of the secessionists. The town council and several prominent townspeople signed a letter to Admiral Du Pont requesting more troops for the defense of the town. When the United States abandoned Jacksonville a few days later, the St. Augustine Unionists, fearing a like fate, requested to be taken aboard the Federal gunboat in the harbor. The navy commander assured them that this would be done, if it became necessary.[40]

Although the military situation would remain uncertain for another month, the Federals put more troops into St. Augustine and affirmed their commitment to permanent occupation of the town. Four companies of the Fourth New Hampshire that had been withdrawn from Jacksonville were disembarked in St. Augustine. Field artillery was hurriedly placed on top of the fort to command the northern approach to town. On April 12 Colonel Bell declared martial law and dissolved the town government, saying that the people had requested outright military rule.[41]

As time passed the Union troops made improvements on the town's defenses. A little way north of the fort an entrenchment was dug from North River across to the San Sebastian River, walling off from the interior the peninsula on which the town was situated. Large cannon were mounted on the fort, and trees were cut down to create an open field of fire. The San Sebastian bridge at King Street, the only entrance to town from the west, was guarded by pickets. The troops were largely quartered in and around St. Francis Barracks at the southern end of town, although some would occupy tents on the terreplein of the fort. Several times the soldiers were sent scurrying through the streets during the night by false alarms of enemy attack. However, the Confederates had no intention of attacking St. Augustine and remained far away on the other side of the St. Johns River.[42]

Although it was impossible to prevent the local inhabitants from

---

39. Du Pont to Welles, 25 March 1862, ORN I: 12, 657; Wright to Col. Louis Bell, 27 March 1862, ORA I: 6, 255-56; Wright to Capt. Louis H. Pelouze, 28 March 1862, ORA I: 6, 256.

40. G. A. Pacetti *et al.* to Du Pont, 25 March 1862, ORN I: 12, 659-60; Nicholson to Du Pont, 17 April 1862, ORN I: 12, 753-54.

41. Bell to Brig. Gen. H. W. Benham, 15 April 1862, ORA I: 14, 333-34.

42. Onville Upton to sister, 26 September 1862, photocopy, Miscellaneous File, St. Augustine History, Civil War Period, Society Library; Justus Silliman to mother (Martha Ann Mitchell Silliman), 6 May 1864, photocopy, Miscellaneous File, St. Augustine History, Civil War Period, Society Library; *St. Augustine Examiner*, 24 October 1868; *St. Augustine News*, 8 February 1891; Henry F. W. Little, *Seventh Regiment, New Hampshire Volunteers in the War of the Rebellion* (Concord, Seventh New Hampshire Veterans Association, 1896), 77; *St. Augustine Evening Record*, 30 April 1977.

communicating with the enemy in the interior, Bell expressed satisfaction with the behavior of most of the natives. Lt. J. W. A. Nicholson, commander of the gunboat anchored in the harbor, concurred: "Most of the men appear to be well disposed, while many of the ladies are becoming to be ladylike, while others are still bitter toward the defenders of that flag under which they have enjoyed such prosperity."[43]

The young men of the Fourth New Hampshire were received by the townspeople reasonably well, but they earned a reputation for lack of discipline. Fanny Williams, a rebel sympathizer who was soon after sent, with her sister Eliza, to an aunt in central Florida, described them as "composed partly of boys from the hills of New Hampshire, great gawky fellows like our 'Crackers,' and partly of foreigners from the mill districts, many of whom could not speak English." However, she felt pity for them since some were suffering from scurvy. Her mother, Mrs. William Henry Williams, gladly traded lemons from her yard in exchange for food.[44] Other soldiers prowled around at night helping themselves to fruit and vegetables from backyard gardens and breaking into unoccupied houses to steal furniture and housewares.[45]

Food, or rather the lack of it, would remain a problem of paramount importance in St. Augustine at times throughout the war. When the Federals arrived, some in town were on the verge of starvation. One recent archeological study indicates that during the Civil War years the occupants of the dig site had reverted to a subsistence diet much like that prevailing 300 years earlier when the Spanish settlers were eking out an existence from the land.[46] The conquering Yankees saved the situation by opening their commissary and distributing food to the destitute inhabitants.[47] Even die-hard secessionists traded with the troops for food. Mrs. Joseph Lee Smith, the mother of Confederate General Edmund Kirby Smith, bought sugar and bacon from some soldiers who appeared on her doorstep—and then wrote in her journal, "I never expected to deal with these men. . . ."[48]

The return of St. Augustine to United States governance posed a problem for those who had sincerely transferred their allegiance to the Confederacy. Some had departed town before the arrival of the Federal troops and would live out the war exiled in central Florida towns such as Lake City and Monticello. Most, however, remained in town. They now found it necessary to behave circumspectly, just as the Unionists

43. Nicholson to Du Pont, 8 April 1862, ORN I: 12, 723-24; Wright to Bell, 8 April 1862, ORA I: 6, 129-30.

44. Recollections of Fanny Williams Carmen, Miscellaneous File, St. Augustine History, Civil War Period, Society Library.

45. Jenckes to Reid, 26 May 1862; A. Anderson to George Burt, 8 July 1862 and James W. Allen to George Burt, 9 September 1862, Burt Papers, MC 2, Society Library.

46. Charles R. Ewen, "Excavations at the Ximénez-Fatio House" (Submitted to the Florida Chapter of the Colonial Dames in America, April 1984, mimeographed), 111-112.

47. Bell to Benham, 15 April 1862, ORA I: 14, 334; Rodgers to Du Pont, 12 March 1862, ORN I: 12, 595; Du Pont to Welles, 3 May 1862, ORN I: 12, 708-09; *St. Augustine Examiner*, 9 April 1862.

48. Journal of Mrs. Joseph Lee Smith, 6 May 1862, Biographical File, Joseph Lee Smith, Society Library.

had been obliged to do during the year when St. Augustine had been a part of the Confederacy. Rebel sympathizer Hannah Jenckes put it clearly: "These times will work wonders, make some of us discreet, and stayers at home. We are beginning the game of rise Ladies and change places, and between two stools your humble servant is coming to the ground."[49]

From the start the Federal authorities had issued oaths of allegiance to the United States to any residents willing to swear their loyalty. True Unionists did so willingly. Soon the army began to use the pressure of hunger to induce oath taking from the others. Secessionists judged it cruel to starve women and children into submission, but the Federals felt it incongruous that they should be obliged to feed the families of Confederate soldiers fighting to destroy the Union. One observed, "Nearly all the inhabitants who remained were dependent at once upon the Federal commissary for rations, and they were not backward in making applications for relief to a government they pretended to despise; but they were obliged to take an oath of allegiance to the United States before their wants were supplied."[50]

Rev. L. R. Staudenmayer, the Episcopal minister, explained that he and others had taken the oath under protest. "I had no option," he declared, "except being placed beyond the pickets leaving Mrs. Staudenmayer's and my own property to be robbed by the enemy. Besides, I was anxious to protect the Church and Rectory against Yankee pollution. . . ."[51] However, because Staudenmayer agreed to cooperate with the Federals, he became the object of a movement by his secessionist parishioners to oust him from the church. Ultimately the Union officers decided to expel him, probably as a source of contention in the community, and he was sent into the Confederate lines.[52]

Following the capture of several Confederate deserters found hiding in town and the assassination of Unionists in the area by rebel guerillas, the Federal authorities in the Department of the South ordered the expulsion of all rebel sympathizers from St. Augustine. In September bills were posted around town ordering all persons over the age of fourteen to attend a meeting at the Presbyterian Church. Colonel Bell was, by this time, heartily disliked by many, and the calling of this meeting inflamed the emotions of the secessionists. Victoria Williams, Fannie's sister, recalled, after the war, that at the meeting "one of the officers made a disgusting speech, he had been drinking." Following speeches

49. Jenckes to Reid, 26 May 1862.

50. Smith Journal, 7 May 1862; Rev. L. R. Staudenmayer to George R. Fairbanks, August 1862, Fairbanks Papers; Little, 69; Anonymous, *History of Company K of the Seventh Connecticut Volunteers* (n. p. 1910), 78.

51. Staudenmayer to Fairbanks, August 1862, Fairbanks Papers.

52. Jenckes to Reid, 10 March 1862; F. K. Smith to George R. Burt, no date, Burt Papers; F. K. Smith to Staudenmayer, 30 April 1862, Burt Papers; Maj. Charles G. Halpine to Bell, 20 June 1862, ORA I: 14, 356-57.

National Archives.

United States Provost Guard House, December 6, 1864, (present day Government House) seen from the plaza at King and St. George streets.

by several Union officers, all those who would agree to take the oath of allegiance were led to three places in the church where they could lay their hands on a Bible and swear to be loyal to the United States and to inform the authorities of any seditious activities in town.[53]

Mary Catherine Genovar, who was among the crowd that day, remembered being frightened and confused. As she pondered what to do a man in the church whispered, "You don't have to keep it. Say you will or they'll shut you up." Fearful of the punishment threatened by the Federals, she took the oath.[54]

Victoria Williams was among those who refused to take the oath and who stayed in the church for hours. These recalcitrant women and their children were told that they would be expelled immediately. Victoria and her mother hastily gave their family valuables to a Federal officer with whom they had made friends, realizing that their house would be ransacked as soon as they departed. "With only the clothes they had on, and maybe a small bundle hastily gathered," the rebel women and children were hurried aboard the decrepit transport ship *Burnside* and sent toward Jacksonville. "The horrors of that boat no words can describe," testified Victoria. The ship leaked, and in the dark hold many were seasick from the heavy ocean swells. Mrs. Williams discovered that the Federal officer to whom she gave her valuables had secretly returned some of them in a pillow which he handed her as they departed.[55]

When the *Burnside* arrived off the Jacksonville bar she was met by another ship carrying Gen. Alfred H. Terry, who held orders countermanding the order to expel the rebel sympathizers. The *Burnside* returned to St. Augustine, but since many of the women had sold all their possessions, they could not stay in St. Augustine and shortly went beyond the lines to seek aid in the Confederacy. They were encouraged to go in order to reduce the number of mouths to feed in town. Victoria and her mother were among those who stayed in town.[56]

At this time the Fourth New Hampshire was replaced by the Seventh New Hampshire, commanded by Col. H. S. Putnam. The arriving Yankees were served a welcoming banquet on the plaza by their departing kinsmen. Colonel Putnam would prove to be more sympathetic to the townspeople, and was remembered as a "kind-hearted, true gentleman."[57] When he was killed a year later in the assault on Fort Wagner, outside Charleston, the people of St. Augustine were saddened by his death.[58]

53. Halpine to Bell, 20 June 1862, ORA I: 14, 356-57; B. E. Carr to George Burt, 7 September 1862, Burt Papers; Recollections of Victoria Williams Smith, Biographical File, Samuel Williams, Society Library.
54. "The Grandmother of Charlotte Street," typed mss., Biographical File, Genovar, Society Library; *St. Augustine Record*, 30 April 1912.
55. Smith Recollections; Carmen Recollections.
56. Brig. Gen. Alfred H. Terry to Maj. W. P. Prentice, 23 September 1862, ORA I: 14, 386.
57. Lt. Edwin W. Smith, General Orders No. 27, 17 August 1862, ORA I: 14, 376; Little, 66-67; *St. Augustine Record*, 30 April 1912.
58. *St. Augustine Record*, 30 April 1912.

At the end of January 1863, another order came to expel all in St. Augustine who had sons or husbands in the rebel army. This time the expulsion was carried out in a more orderly manner. A ship bearing refugees was sent north on February 2 and then again on February 9. The Williams women set forth once again and Victoria recalled that Colonel Putnam refused to allow Negro troops to guard the women and children on the transport and sent some men of the Seventh New Hampshire. On the voyage, Victoria became involved in an argument with a much disliked officer, Col. Liberty Billings, over his avowed abolitionist sentiments. At Fernandina the Williams women and a group of others were put off. Confederate cavalry escorting a train of oxcarts met them and, in a cold pouring rain, set off for Lake City. The steamer continued north, dropping off groups of women and children at several Southern ports.[59]

Other individuals and small groups would be expelled at various times for the remainder of the war. Some of those who were forced out protested that they were loyal to the Union, even though their sons or brothers were serving in the Confederate army. They argued that their relatives had been drafted against their will. Justified or not, cruel or not, the expulsions further depopulated the town. Just after the second expulsion one of those left behind wrote, "the glory of this town has disappeared. The streets are deserted."[60]

Following the dramatic events surrounding the expulsions of September 1862 and February 1863, relations between the soldiers and townspeople settled down. As new units of the United States Army were rotated into the town, replacing departing units, the soldiers encountered a stable situation. The white population had been reduced to a few hundred, mostly women. The Minorcans especially avoided contact. "They are generally secessionists and keep themselves aloof from the officers and soldiers," reported one trooper. The soldiers referred to them as "Sugar Cane and Mullet" or "United States Paupers."[61]

The small band of Unionists in town provide a semblance of civilian society for the occupying Yankees. Soldiers and officers mixed socially with the Unionists, mostly ladies, who were glad to have the company of sympathetic spirits. Mrs. Clarissa Anderson, a well-to-do grove owner, frequently invited officers to her home where they found "a charming atmosphere of culture and refinement." Eventually some offi-

59. *Ibid.*; Smith Recollections; C. Anderson to A. Anderson, 24 January 1863, Anderson Papers; Little, 91.

60. Anonymous, 103; Alfred S. Roe, *Twenty-Fourth Regiment, Massachusetts Volunteers, 1861-1866* (Worcester, Twenty-Fourth Veterans Association, 1907), 272; *Fernandina Peninsula*, 4 June 1863; P. J. Staudenraus, "A War Correspondent's View of St. Augustine and Fernandina: 1863," *Florida Historical Quarterly* 41 (July 1962): 61-62; Valentine Chamberlain to friend, 18 February 1863, P. K. Yonge Library of Florida History.

61. Roe, 236; Worthington C. Ford, ed., *War Letters, 1862-1865 of John Chipman Gray and John Codman Ropes* (Boston, Houghton Mifflin Co., 1927), 334-35; Blaky Mason to Frank, 24 April 1863, Miscellaneous File, St. Augustine History, Civil War Period, Society Library.

cers brought their wives down from the North, a few boarding in the home of Sarah Mather, a Yankee schoolmistress. The Unionists were invited guests at the military's band concerts, glee club programs, and stage show presentations. The soldiers were also pleased to hear female voices singing in their church services. In a more serious vein, the Union sympathizers could serve as go-betweens for the troops in their relations with disaffected townspeople.[62]

Because of their knowledge of the local geography native Unionists were sometimes used as scouts or guides for the Federal troops when they ventured into the countryside. This was a risky enterprise for the Unionists since the Confederates had special hatred for those they regarded as turncoats and spies. United States Army Pvt. Onville Upton reported that on one military sweep through the countryside "the Postmaster and another man went as a guide they were awful fraid of being taken they kept very clost to us." The postmaster was probably the same "Yankee postmaster" who had been identified soon after the occupation of St. Augustine as one of the "few traitors in town" by a Confederate sympathizer.[63]

For the first two years of Union occupation the major reason for incursions into the interior seems to have been foraging for cattle and hogs to support the garrison's and townspeople's diet. The army commissary was the primary source of basic foodstuffs for townspeople and soldiers alike. The army had developed a schedule of distribution for families and doled out basic staples such as hardtack, bacon, cornmeal, peas, candles, soap, and salt to the local inhabitants. However, as late as 1864 the town suffered from want of food when supply ships failed to arrive. Fish, chickens, and fresh fruit were available locally to supplement the government rations. At the San Sebastian bridge there were regular trading days when rebel "crackers" from the countryside could come in to trade foodstuffs with the St. Augustinians. One basic wartime food was corn pone made from a mixture of government issue hardtack and locally produced corn meal.[64]

George Burt and B. E. Carr, two local Unionist merchants, gained permission from Federal authorities to reopen trade with the North. Their stores constituted an alternative source of supplies for those with hard United States currency. Even then, some luxury items such as

62. *St. Augustine Examiner*, 16 April 1862; H. W. L. Hawley to John Peck, 22 June 1863, Burt Papers; newspaper clipping, 7 January 1895, Anderson Papers; C. Anderson to A. Anderson, 23 November 1864, Anderson Papers; Silliman to mother, 19 April 1864; James M. Nichols, *Perry's Saints* [Fourty-Eighth New York Volunteers] (Boston, D. Lothrop and Co., 1886), 180; Roe, 236-39.

63. Upton to mother, 13 March 1863; Staudenmayer to Fairbanks, 16 August 1862, Fairbanks Papers; Roe, 256-57.

64. C. Anderson to A. Anderson, 26 December 1863, 19 February 1864, Anderson Papers; Schedule of Rations, Biographical File, William Burr Jones, Society Library; Little, 75; Ford, 334-35; Roe, 238-39; *St. Augustine Record*, 30 April 1912.

National Archives.

Commissary Store House, December 11, 1864, at the corner of Charlotte and Cathedral streets. The cathedral is in the background on the right.

coffee, apples, and Irish potatoes remained scarce and much sought-after items.[65]

Carr, elderly and nearly deaf, was a popular figure in soldier society. His store was a gathering place, and it was reputed that Carr could find any item in its inventory. Justus Silliman of the Seventeenth Connecticut described it thus: "It is a large establishment, principly hardware it has the appearance of having been in operation since the year one I spent an hour in there the other day looking at the ancient specimins of hardware."[66]

News from the outside world was a scarce item. The supply ship from Hilton Head, which came every two or three weeks, was the most regular source of information, but even this ship could not always be relied upon to appear on schedule. A newspaper correspondent who came in on the courier ship declared, "One can fancy that this staid, sleepy and ancient town of St. Augustine is a part of another planet." Sometimes a rebel at the San Sebastian bridge would bring in a Southern newspaper to trade. Although events described in arriving news sources were sometimes more than a month old, word of great battles or momentous events created just as great a sensation as if they had occurred recently. Perhaps the reaction was even heightened because of the anticipation built up by delay.[67]

Despite the isolation and occasional short rations, St. Augustine was considered a desirable duty station by the Union soldiers. A writer from the Seventh Connecticut expressed a typical view when he stated: "On the whole the period of about two months spent by the regiment at St. Augustine was looked upon as one of the easiest times of its service." When the Seventh shipped out of town, one of their replacements observed: "Many of them surely repented ever having enlisted. they all appeared glum at the prospect of going to Virginia."[68]

With little fighting to do, after drills and guard duty the soldiers found that they had plenty of time for recreation. Many went sailing or canoeing on the bay, and some tried their luck fishing. Hunting excursions into the pine woods were less common because of the danger from rebel guerillas. Some soldiers managed to capture "marsh tackies," the little wild ponies found in the area, and tame them as personal mounts. Flirting with the local girls was common. Sometimes it led to punishment by the officers, and in at least one case it led to marriage.[69]

The Yankee soldiers were invariably impressed by the appearance

65. Burt Papers, 1862-1865; A. Anderson to Aunt Kate, 4 September 1863, Anderson Papers; Little, 89.
66. Silliman to mother, 6 May 1864.
67. Smith Journal, 7 May 1862; *New York Daily Tribune*, 16 August 1862; *Fernandina Peninsula*, 13 August 1863; Staudenraus, 61-62; William Burr Jones to father, 7 November 1864.
68. Silliman to mother, 19 April 1864; Stephen Walkley, *History of the Seventh Connecticut Volunteer Infantry* (1905?), 68.
69. "The Grandmother of Charlotte Street;" A. Anderson to George Burt, 8 July 1862, Burt Papers; Diary of James H. Linsley, 50-55, P. K. Yonge Library; Upton to sister, 26 September 1862; Little, 66-88.

National Archives.

Post Quarter Master's, December 11, 1864, at the corner of Cathedral Street and Avenida Menendez. B. E. Carr's store is the second building on the right and the third building is Carr's house (present-day Chart House restaurant).

of St. Augustine and filled their letters home with descriptions of the locale. "This is the strangest and most romantic looking town I was ever in," went one typical comment. The reputed "Oldest House in the United States" stood on the bayfront just south of the plaza, its wooden parts having been removed and its stone disappearing in small pieces as Northern boys chipped away bits of coquina to take back home. The soldiers also purchased souvenirs, such as palm leaf goods, from the locals. One enterprising man sold canes carved from the wood, he said, from the oldest house.[70]

The major complaint the townspeople made against the soldiers was their petty pilfering. They broke into abandoned houses to take items which would make life in the barracks more comfortable for themselves. Chickens and fruit regularly disappeared from back yards. More seriously, fires in empty houses occurred with alarming frequency. Most of these seem to have been accidental, but some were probably arson. Establishment of a 9 P.M. curfew and placement of picket stations along the streets after nightfall helped to reduce nocturnal excursions.[71]

In the fall of 1863 St. Augustine became a convalescent camp where soldiers could recover from the rigors of fighting on the front lines. Rather than evacuating troops to the cold North, the army had decided to send them to Florida, which already had a reputation as a winter health resort. Construction of the hospital stirred up activity in town. Unemployed men found work in carpentry, and those with henhouses and gardens found a ready market for their produce. Before the war St. Augustine had made a living from sick Yankees, and now it was back in the old business.[72]

The garrison seldom had opportunity to engage the Confederates in combat since their job was simply to defend St. Augustine if the enemy attacked, which the rebels had no intention of doing. However, shortly after the occupation of town, the Confederates did raise a cavalry unit from the Ocala region commanded by Capt. J. J. Dickison. The purpose of this force was to patrol the area west of the St. Johns River watching for Federal incursions and, occasionally, to harass the Federals occupying St. Augustine. Because of Dickison's presence the Union troops usually stayed inside the town's defensive perimeter. Some of the few who ventured out into the countryside ended up as Dickison's prisoners.[73]

In March 1863, Dickison slipped across the St. Johns to stage an ambush of the woodcutters sent to the forest north of town to procure

70. Silliman to mother, 25 April 1864.

71. C. Anderson to A. Anderson, 7 April 1863, 15 October 1864, Anderson Papers; Little, 69-90.

72. C. Anderson to A. Anderson, 15 October, 9 November, 14 November 1863, 11, 25, 26 January 1864, Anderson Papers; *Fernandina Peninsula*, 29 October 1863.

73. Little, 89; Mary Elizabeth Dickison, *Dickison and His Men* (Louisville, Courier Journal Job Printing Co., 1890), 17, 87.

firewood. However, Colonel Putnam detected the rebels and attempted to spring a trap of his own by sending three companies of the Seventh New Hampshire out to the area of Fort Peyton, southwest of town, to cut off Dickison's line of retreat. The Yankees found Dickison's base camp and exchanged fire with the rebels in an area of thick palmettoes and pines. Dickison escaped to the west. Neither side had suffered any casualties in the skirmish, although five Union scouts were captured. After the fight Private Upton of the Seventh wrote home that this was the most "fun" and excitement he had experienced in Florida and declared that all his comrades were ready to chase Dickison again.[74]

The Federals got their chance in December when Dickison returned to attempt the ambush a second time. This time he was successful. While advancing through dense palmetto thickets, the forward guard of the woodcutters was surprised and routed, leaving their commanding officer mortally wounded. Dickison rounded up twenty-four prisoners and hurried back across the St. Johns with the Federal infantry in distant pursuit. "A most unfortunate affair," concluded James Linsley of the Tenth Connecticut.[75]

The skirmishes with Dickison were typical of the style of fighting in east Florida: small units, hit-and-run, limited objectives. However, January 1864 saw the stirrings of a major military enterprise by the Federals. The United States government had decided to attempt the conquest and reconstruction of the northern part of the state, a goal which seemed attainable given the absence of adequate Confederate defenses.

In St. Augustine the Tenth Connecticut and Twenty-fourth Massachusetts received orders to join the Federal expedition, leaving behind only two companies to hold the town. The little array of musicians, clerks, and untrained recruits left in town were instructed to lock themselves in the fort if threatened.[76] When news of the subsequent defeat at Olustee arrived in St. Augustine, there was consternation among the soldiers and Unionists. Confidence in an easy victory turned to fear that the rebels would march into the town itself.[77]

However, despite losing the only major battle of the war in Florida, Union forces continued on the offensive. After the arrival in St. Augustine of the Seventeenth Connecticut in April 1864, the area controlled by the Federal troops was expanded beyond the limits of the town itself. Picolata was garrisoned and patrols scoured the area east of the St. Johns River from Jacksonville south to Volusia. Residents were freed

74. Dickison, 47-48; Col. H. S. Putnam to Halpine, 12 March 1863, ORA I: 14, 224; Upton to sister, 13 March 1863.

75. Linsley Diary, 30 December 1863; Roe, 249; Col. F. A. Osborn to Brig. Gen. J. W. Turner, 1 January 1864, ORA I: 28, 752-53; "Report of Capt. J. J. Dickison, Second Florida Cavalry," ORA I: 28, 753-54.

76. Maj. Gen. Q. A. Gillmore to Osborn, 12 February 1864, ORA I: 35, part 1, 479; Gen. Truman Seymour to Gillmore, 17 February 1864, ORA I: 35, part 1, 284-85; J. L. Otis to Turner, 22 February 1864, ORA I: 35, part 1, 489.

77. C. Anderson to A. Anderson, 15, 23 February, 4 March 1864, Anderson Papers.

from the constraints on their activities which had been enforced in the previous two years. A semblance of normal life was returning.[78]

After two years in residence at St. Francis Barracks, the soldiers had made themselves a comfortable home. Justus Silliman wrote his mother, "The Officers qrs are upstairs they have green blinds to their windows and have taken possession of all the old sofas tables etc and live in style." The enlisted men were given free run of the town when off duty, and, as Private Silliman observed, the officers were inclined "to let us enjoy ourselves so long as we act decently. . . . I believe they all intend to be less rigid than heretofore." The Connecticut private also observed that his commander, Col. William H. Noble, could be seen riding outside town in a carriage with "several gaily dressed young ladies."[79]

So lax did the United States forces become that in December 1864, Colonel Noble was captured by a small band of rebels while riding in his carriage from St. Augustine to Jacksonville. Noble was accompanied only by an aide and neither man was armed. Despite this embarassing incident, the Federals failed to tighten security. A month later a party of soldiers was taken by Dickison's men while attending a dance at the home of a Minorcan woman 12 miles in the country. Another group of 40 became Dickison's prisoners when they ventured to the area of Welaka in search of cotton.[80]

The lives of St. Augustine's black inhabitants underwent a transformation during the war. Just a month before the Battle of Olustee, on January 1, 1864, St. Augustine's black populace celebrated "Emancipation Day," the first anniversary of Lincoln's Emancipation Proclamation. The Freedman's Society sponsored a grand barbecue on the plaza. The army band played "Hail Columbia" and "John Brown's Body," and children from the recently established freedman's school sang spirituals. White chaplains and Negro preachers put their blessings on the occasion. To the several hundred blacks and whites in the crowd that day it seemed that a new day had dawned for the former slaves.[81]

From the start of the war, blacks had hoped and assumed that the conflict would end slavery, despite the United States government's early promises to the South that it would leave slavery intact. The Federals had a problem keeping this promise because wherever United States troops went in the South the slaves flocked to their lines seeking freedom. In the summer of the first year of fighting, Congress had declared that slaves might be seized as "contraband of war."

78. *Ibid.*, 29 April, 3, 9 May 1864; Ford, 334-35.

79. Silliman to mother, 19, 24 April 1864.

80. Edward Marcus, ed., *A New Canaan Private in the Civil War* (New Canaan, New Canaan Historical Society, 1984), 88-89; C. Anderson to A. Anderson, 1 February 1865, Anderson Papers; "District of Florida, 5 February 1865," ORA I, 47, 166.

81. C. Anderson to A. Anderson, 1 January 1864, Anderson Papers; Linsley Diary, 1 January 1864; Roe, 251-52; *St. Augustine Evening Record*, 14 February 1930; Johns, 149-50; Jerrell Shofner, *Nor Is It Over Yet* (Gainesville, University Presses of Florida, 1974), 15.

St. Augustine Historical Society.

United States Barracks at the corner of Charlotte and St. Francis streets, looking north on Charlotte Street. The barracks is on the right and across St. Francis Street from it is the Tovar House.

Soon after Federal occupation of St. Augustine runaway slaves began appearing in town asking for protection. Lieutenant Nicholson had written asking Flag Officer Du Pont for instructions on handling this: "Several contrabands have delivered themselves to, or been arrested by, the guard at the entrance of the city; they have fled from their masters, who are in rebellion. I have sent them to the fort. . . ."[82] Three weeks later the army's Colonel Bell was writing his superior asking what to do with the ever-increasing numbers of blacks entering the lines. He had turned some away from the fort. Gen. David Hunter at Hilton Head responded by declaring all slaves free, but President Lincoln countermanded this order. However, in 1863 came his Emancipation Proclamation.[83]

The possibility of arming the slaves for the defense of St. Augustine had been raised as early as the summer of 1862, and by December of that year blacks from the town were being recruited into the United States Army. In the spring of 1863 one observer noted that most of the able-bodied black men had been carried away to the fighting front. Later, as the war progressed, black troops would become a familiar sight in St. Augustine.[84]

By late 1863 and early 1864 the streets of St. Augustine were walked also by large numbers of refugees coming in from the countryside. Some were Unionists who took the opportunity to flee the South as the Confederacy began to crumble.[85] Most, however, were former rebels who had decided to quit the war. At least one local man slipped quietly into town and rejoined his wife. He was identified as a rebel deserter, jailed, and sent to Hilton Head, as were those who came in and refused to take the oath of allegiance.[86]

While the population of the town increased, other signs of normal order appeared. In the spring of 1864 the Federal District Court was reopened in St. Augustine. Schools reappeared. Miss Julia Colt went from house to house and enlisted twenty young scholars from among the refugee families. The Catholic church and Sunday schools run by Protestant ladies were well attended. Even St. Augustine's orange groves, blighted for nearly three decades by disease, re-emerged under the care of the refugees to fill the town with the aroma of their blossoms.[87]

In order to build support for the Union among those living in areas controlled by the United States, the government devised a means of confiscating the property of rebels and transferring it to Unionists. A

82. Nicholson to Du Pont, 21 March 1862, ORN I: 12, 643.

83. Bell to Benham, 15 April 1862, ORA I: 14, 334; Johns, 150.

84. Halpine to Bell, 20 June 1862, ORA I: 14, 356; Upton to sister, 22 December 1862; C. Anderson to A. Anderson, 24 January, 9 April 1863, Anderson Papers.

85. Roe, 248; Anonymous, 103.

86. C. Anderson to A. Anderson, 15, 27 January, 16 February 1864, Anderson Papers; Silliman to mother, 19, 24 April 1864.

87. *Jacksonville Peninsula*, 14 April 1864; C. Anderson to A. Anderson, 3 November 1864, Anderson Papers.

direct tax was levied on property, which would not be paid if the owner were a rebel on the Confederate side of the lines. This property could then be condemned and sold at auction.[88]

The process of assessing property, collecting the tax, and proceeding against rebel owners took place throughout 1863, and by December the condemned property was ready for auction. Some St. Augustine Unionists looked for ways of saving the property of their rebel friends, but Tax Commissioner Lyman Stickney refused to allow anyone to pay taxes on behalf of a rebel property owner. Therefore when the auction occurred late in December some individuals purchased the houses and lots of rebels with the intention of holding them for the owners until after the war.[89]

A considerable amount of property changed hands, some going to Union soldiers, some to freed slaves, and some to recent arrivals in town. The sales altered the lives of many old-time residents and provided grounds for extended litigation following the war.[90]

At the same time as the tax sales the United States attempted to organize a new state government under the terms of President Lincoln's "Ten Percent Plan" of reconstruction. Lincoln sent his secretary, John Hay, to East Florida to collect oaths of loyalty from the necessary 1,100 men (representing ten percent of the 1860 voters). On December 19 a meeting was held in the St. Augustine court house to arrange for a state constitutional convention which was proposed for March 1. Tax Commissioner Stickney, who might be regarded as the area's first carpetbagger, called the meeting to order. Judge David R. Dunham, one of those who had met the invading Yankees on the seawall in March 1862, was elected chairman. The meeting passed resolutions calling for the abolition of slavery, disfranchisement of rebels, and re-establishment of normal relations with the United States. However, the subsequent defeat of the army at Olustee ended hopes of implementing this program. The March 1 convention was never held, and Hay returned north.[91]

The Confederate victory at Olustee only postponed the return of Florida to the Union. The war continued in east Florida in its usual pattern, with no major military engagements for another year. However, so normal had conditions become in St. Augustine that when news of Lee's surrender came, there was little impact on life in town. Even the celebration of victory was muted, for the packet boat which brought news of Lee's surrender also bore word of Lincoln's assassination.[92]

The process of reconstruction which had begun in March of 1862

88. Shofner, 5.

89. *Fernandina Peninsula*, 30 April 1863; John Peck to George Burt, 16 November 1863, Burt Papers; C. Anderson to A. Anderson, 11, 18 December 1863, Anderson Papers.

90. C. Anderson to A. Anderson, 21 December 1863, Anderson Papers; Shofner, 15.

91. Oath signed by George Burt, 16 February 1864, Burt Papers; Shofner, 8-9; *Fernandina Peninsula*, 24 December 1863.

92. C. Anderson to A. Anderson, 8 May 1865, Anderson Papers.

would continue after the war. Soon Yankee tourists and settlers would arrive in town in larger numbers than before the war, and the railroad would knit St. Augustine more closely than ever into the Union. The spirit of Southern nationalism would slowly evolve into a sentimental nostalga for the "Lost Cause."

In 1872 the Daughters of the Confederacy, led by Anna Dummett, the rebel patriot who had written the Florida battle songs in 1861, erected a stone obelisk to the memory of the 44 men who died in the war. It remains today as one of the few tangible evidences of St. Augustine's 14-month tenure in the Southern Confederacy.

Fort Marion in Civil War Times

Luis Rafael Arana

On the morning of Friday, April 4, 1986, members of the symposium gathered at the entrance of Castillo de San Marcos for a tour given by Luis R. Arana, the fort's historian. To preserve the atmosphere of the guided tour, his talk and the photographs he displayed are presented as he described each location. The photographs are keyed to the text and the numbers are those used in the photograph collection of the Castillo.

Welcome to Castillo de San Marcos, known as Fort Marion between 1825 and 1942. Before we enter the fort, let me give you some background information about this venerable pile of stone.

There have been fortifications in St. Augustine since the very founding of the city in 1565. Before the building of Castillo de San Marcos, there were nine successive wooden forts beginning in that year and ending 110 years later. Whether of wood or stone, the St. Augustine fortification had two main objectives: (1) the presence of a fort in Florida strengthened the Spanish title to the land, and (2) the effective occupation of the land protected Spanish merchant ships returning to Europe from the Caribbean area, via the route of the Gulf Stream, which, as you know, runs along the east coast of Florida. The objectives became somewhat diluted as circumstances changed with time.

The English settlement of Charleston (South Carolina) in 1670 opened an intense rivalry for control of the southeast of present-day United States, and thus posed a serious threat to the Spanish hold on Florida. Consequently, the Castillo was begun in 1672 and finished in 1695. The features you see here and will see inside are not the original 17th-century look. They are the result of "modernization" work, that is, the replacement of beams by arches in 1738-40 and in 1752-56 to support the terreplein or gundeck, and the replacement of the smaller, original ravelin in 1762.

Florida became British in 1763, and the Castillo, now named Fort St. Marks, protected it during the American Revolution. When the Spanish captured Mobile and then Pensacola in West Florida, the English commander in St. Augustine said that Fort St. Marks made him confident about facing the Spanish or the Americans successfully.

The fort became Spanish again in 1784 and remained so until 1821. During this period, it enabled Spain to transfer Florida to the United States with honor. The War Department received custody of the fortification and soon renamed it Fort Marion, because Castillo de San Marcos

---

Luis Rafael Arana is the historian of Castillo de San Marcos and Fort Matanzas National Monuments.

was apt to be confused with Fort San Marcos in West Florida. The new name honored Francis Marion, South Carolina's guerrilla leader in the Revolutionary War. The construction of the Water Battery in 1842-44 transformed the fort into an active United States coastal defense unit. We shall hear more about the Water Battery later.

The fort is a unique specimen of a vanished style of military architecture and engineering, and the symbol of the 235-year Spanish presence in the southeast of today's United States. It embodies the history of that presence when it had been the principle work of a defense system that locally included supplementary lines, redoubts to the west and Fort Matanzas to the south, and regionally reached out to Fort San Carlos at Fernandina, the Pellicer Fortified House south of Matanzas Inlet, and Buena Vista Redoubt somewhere in Palatka.

Fort Marion was designated a National Monument in 1924 and its custody was transferred to the Department of the Interior, specifically the National Park Service, in 1933. An act of Congress in 1942 restored the original Spanish name.

This Civil War photograph (A-3) shows how the passage of time has changed the south facade of Castillo at which we are looking. It was taken sometime between 1862 and 1865 by Sam A. Cooley, a photographer accredited to the Union army's Department of the South. There was more plaster on the south wall then than there is now, the quarters of the Spanish coat of arms above the gate are outlined more sharply, and the bridge railing has a more primitive look. The soldiers standing in the gun embrasures are wearing capes over their uniforms. Let us now go inside the fort.

Here, at the south side of the courtyard, we look at another Cooley photograph (A-18). Notice that the facade of the chapel is almost completely decayed. The present facade is a reconstruction made in 1915. To the left of the two piles of cannonballs in the middle, there is an ammunition field cart, and to the right, a field piece limber or two-wheeled gun transport. At the top, on the north terreplein, you can see the type of lodgement used by the Union soldiers. In World War II this type of shelter was called a hutment, and consisted of a tent-shaped wooden room covered by a tent. The wooden room was slightly smaller than the tent, so that the latter fitted snugly over the former. There were hutments in the Water Battery too, according to a history of the Seventh New Hampshire Volunteer Regiment.

Now, look first at the arch supporting the stairway in that southeast corner, and then at this third Cooley photograph (A-35). To the left, abutting the arch, there is a tall, masonry feature which Edwin C. Bearss, the National Park Service chief historian, is unable to explain in his study of the Castillo during the 1821-1933 period. From one side of the photo to the other, you can also see a clothesline over which a pair of trousers and a white garment are draped. The latter might be a pair of longjohns. Stacked under the arch, there are six of the 21 guns left by the Spaniards in 1821. Hutments were erected on the east terreplein too, but all covering tents cannot be seen clearly.

This photograph (A-2), taken probably shortly after the end of the Civil War by another photographer, bears comparison to and contrast with the Cooley photos A-18 and A-35. The stacks of cannonballs are still there, but the gun limber is gone. The height of the feature abutting the stairway arch is lower, as if there had been some razing. The hutments on the east terreplein are still standing but are not covered by tents, which may imply that most of the troops had been removed. A segment of the courtyard wall above the room in the middle is missing.

This other photograph (A-12) seems to have been taken the same day as A-2, probably by the same photographer. The details here, not shown in the previous photo, are the six unserviceable Spanish guns under the arch, the jib crane with brace over the parapet toward the left, and, had the photo been in color, the navy blue coat and sky blue pants of the Union uniform worn by the soldier on the right.

"Was the stairway arch shaped that way because it had to support the weight of guns being taken up to the terreplein?" a tour participant asks.

"No. Unless the gun was very short, it would have been very difficult to make the left turn at the first landing (see A-35), then continue up to the second landing, and finally make the right turn onto the terreplein. The Spaniards, and probably the Americans too, hauled their big guns upstairs by placing two long, foot-square beams parallel to each other, the lower ends on the courtyard ground and, after knocking out a segment of courtyard wall parapet (see A-2), the upper ends on the terreplein edge, then spanning the beams with boards. This in effect provided an inclined plane to pull the guns up by using the proper rig of block and tackle. The arch and the stairway supported by it were built about 1756, and probably rebuilt once before they got as worn out as shown in photo A-35. The present arch and stairway were rebuilt in 1886."

"Is there water still in the well?" another participant asks.

"The well at the southwest corner of the courtyard still contains water, but it is not good water. There is documentary mention that the well was cleaned several times because the water had become brackish."

We have now come up to the east terreplein of Fort Marion, where we can look down on the Water Battery. The 20-gun work was built in 1842-44 by 1st Lieutenant Henry W. Benham of the Corps of Engineers, who, during the Civil War, was for a time the brigadier general commanding the Northern District of the Department of the South. When the lone custodian surrendered the fort to the Confederates on January 7, 1861, the battery held four 8-inch siege howitzers and sixteen 32-pounder smooth bore cannons. Confederate strategists soon resolved to

A–3

A–18

A–35

A–2

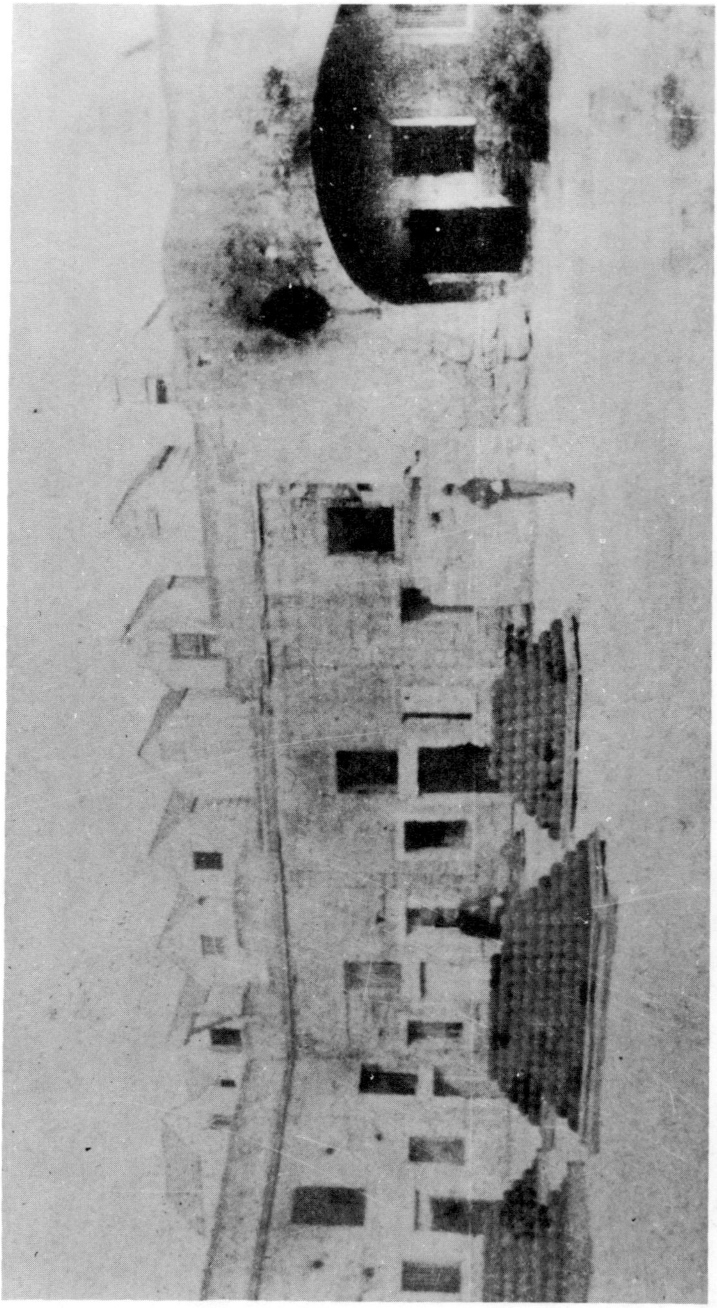

A–12

Fort Marion.

St Augustine, Florida.

A–964

A–142

A–141

A–1

A–3351

fight in Tennessee and Virginia, letting coast line landings go unchallenged unless penetration inland was attempted. By May the howitzers and twelve 32-pounders had been shipped to the fighting fronts.

St. Augustine came under Union control in March 1862. Soon thereafter orders came to strengthen Fort Marion by installing in the fort proper some of the equipment in the Water Battery gun emplacements. First Lieutenant John Alphonse Tardy, an engineer in the Department of the South, was chosen for the job.

Tardy, a New Yorker, had entered the U. S. Military Academy in 1855, and graduated as No. 2 in his class in 1860. He was brevetted second lieutenant of engineers, receiving substantive grade in 1861. Tardy became a first lieutenant on August 6 of the same year, and captain in March 1863. He was brevetted major in 1865, and received that grade in the regular army on March 7, 1867. Tardy's life was short, for he died three months later.

Here's a photograph of an artist's sketch of Fort Marion during the Civil War (A-964). It is companion to a sketch of St. Francis Barracks dated 1863, drawn by the same person who drew this one, and probably done at the same time as the other, judging by the artistic style. The sketch shows two of the four gun locations in Fort Marion during the Civil War. Shown are the cannon in the northwest bastion, and the guns pointing east in the southeast bastion. The caliber of the latter was smaller than that of the guns depicted. Not shown are the cannon at the north parapet of the northeast bastion, and the gun at the gorge (narrow entrance) of the southwest bastion.

We are now at the north parapet of San Carlos (northeast) Bastion of the fort. Before showing proof that a gun was located here, it will be worthwhile to hear part of Lieutenant Tardy's instructions regarding his work in the fort. Those instructions read, "to put such repairs as can be conveniently added for its [St. Augustine's] defense, change traverse circles from the water battery to the interior work [the fort]."

To follow this up, here's a photograph taken in 1939 during the rehabilitation of the terreplein in this bastion (A-142). It shows that a pintle and a traverse circle were once installed at the north parapet. The front of the gun carriage turned on the pintle, and the wheels at the rear rolled on the traverse circle, enabling the gun to cover a sector of 180°. This controlled all the northern land approaches to St. Augustine, and the access of Hospital Creek from the bay. The creek was navigable for small vessels all the way from the North River before the complex of the Florida School for the Deaf and Blind cut it in two.

And this companion photograph (A-141) gives us a clearer view of the pintle and traverse circle, both mounted on granite left over from the Water Battery construction.

We are now in San Pablo (northwest) Bastion, where there was a gun emplaced during the Civil War as shown in photo A-964. This one was positioned soon after the Union army occupied Fort Marion, in order to control the open northern land approach to St. Augustine. The city is on a small peninsula bounded by water on the other three sides. This photograph (A-1) of the fort about 1885 shows that the parapet and the sentry box of San Pablo Bastion were lowered to the height that would accomodate the travel of the gun 180° on its traversing arc. The parapet and the sentry box were restored in 1886 as a result of work authorized by Congress two years earlier, appropriating $5000 for the restoration of Fort Marion. This is the first instance of the use of United States public money for historic preservation.

We have come to the gorge of San Pedro (southwest) Bastion. This photograph (A-3351) taken in 1939 of the terreplein rehabilitation at the gorge shows the concrete platform and pintle of the gun position here. This one controlled the western land approach and several fords in the San Sebastian River. To facilitate the traverse of the piece, here too the parapet in front of the gun, the bastion's northern flanker, and at the west face was lowered, as can be seen in the A-1 1885 fort photo. The platform's height must have been noticeable to all visitors from the end of the Civil War until the terreplein rehabilitation did away with it.

The guns in the San Agustín (southeast) Bastion may not have been solely the heavy pieces depicted in the 1863 sketch of Fort Marion. These seem to have been mounted on the barbette (pintle and traverse arc) carriage, although there is no record or any traces of such emplacements in the locations shown. There are indications that San Agustín contained also a howitzer mounted on a field carriage and another one on a siege carriage.

Tour participants ask questions that prompt additional information. Fort Marion was never taken by force. The lone sergeant custodian in 1861 did not offer resistance to the company of Confederate artillerymen who demanded his surrender. Similarly, there was no action on the return of the Union troops and after. However, there were skirmishes in the outlying areas of St. Augustine. Pickets alerted the town of the presence of approaching Confederates.

The restoration of Fort Marion in 1886 was spurred by retired Colonel Albert Tracy. He wrote that St. Augustine's earlier importance had prompted Union troops to occupy the city during the Civil War, however, its defenses had been allowed to deteriorate. General Q. A. Gillmore was at the time responsible for the condition of Atlantic seacoast forts and he replied that St. Augustine had been occupied to bottle up blockade runners and to establish a hospital due to the good climate. Nevertheless, Gillmore supported Tracy's proposal for restoration. The Spanish named the bastions of the fort, but the Americans used those names in the English language. San Pedro Bastion became St. Peter, San Carlos became St. Charles, San Pablo became St. Paul and San Agustín became St. Augustine. Earlier, the British had also used their language to rename the three redoubts of the Cubo line, the earthwork running from the fort westward to the San Sebastian River. The redoubt closest to the Castillo, Santo Domingo, became Fort Moultrie. The westernmost redoubt, Cubo, became Fort Clarke and the one in between, Medio Cubo, became Fort Tonyn.

In Spanish times, the Castillo walls could absorb cannon balls to a limited depth due to the composition of coquina stone. In the 1850's, however, the development of rifled cannon made stone and brick forts obsolete. During the Civil War, General Gillmore had breached Fort Pulaski and forced it to surrender in less than 48 hours, and had battered Fort Sumter into a ruin. The Castillo was never fired on with rifled cannon; had it been, we might not now have a national monument.

Let's end the tour by stating that at Castillo de San Marcos, formerly Fort Marion, the three-year span of the Civil War in St. Augustine is a miniscule period compared with the 235-year Spanish presence. This makes that war a secondary theme in the historical interpretation of the structure.

Sources

Luis Rafael Arana and Albert Manucy, *The Building of Castillo de San Marcos* Philadelphia: Eastern National Park and Monument Association, 1977.

Frank Barnes, *Fort Sumter National Monument/South Carolina* Washington: National Park Service, 1952.

Edwin C. Bearss and John C. Paige, *Historic Structure Report for Castillo de San Marcos National Monument/St. Johns County/Florida* Denver: National Park Service, 1983.

Omega G. East, "St. Augustine During the Civil War," *Florida Historical Quarterly*, XXXI, No. 2, 75-91.

T. H. S. Hamersly, *Complete Army and Navy Register of the United States of America* New York: 1888.

F. B. Heitman, *Historical Register and Dictionary of the United States Army*, 2 vols. Urbana: University of Illinois Press, 1965.

Ralston B. Lattimore, *Fort Pulaski National Monument/Georgia* Washington: National Park Service, 1954.

H. F. W. Little, *The Seventh Regiment, New Hampshire Volunteers, in the War of the Rebellion* Concord, N. H.: 1896.

Francis T. Miller (ed.), *The Photographic History of the Civil War*, 10 vols. New York: The Review of Reviews, 1911.

Alfred S. Roe, *The Twenty-Fourth Regiment, Massachusetts Volunteers, 1861-1866* Worcester, Mass.: Twenty-Fourth Veteran Association, 1907.

Jorge Vigón, *Historia de la artillería española*, 3 vols. Madrid: Consejo Superior de Investigaciones Científicas, 1947.

Ancient City Defenders: The St. Augustine Blues

David J. Coles

In the late spring of 1860 national disunion seemed imminent. The growing crisis that had threatened the American nation for decades appeared to be on the verge of erupting into armed conflict. Meeting in Charleston, South Carolina in May, the Democratic Party failed to nominate a candidate. Southern delegates stormed from the convention, eventually adopting a strictly sectional platform. The Democratic breakup seemed to assure a Republican victory in the November general election.

Throughout the South, military companies organized against this perceived threat. Floridians were quick to join the call to arms. On May 12, a group of prominent St. Augustine citizens met in the town's City Hall for the purpose of forming a volunteer "minute man" unit to defend the ancient city.[1]

St. Augustine's inhabitants already had a long tradition of military service dating to the first Spanish period. More recently, the town's militia had played an important role in the Second Seminole War of 1835-1842. By the 1850's however, with the Indian threat diminished, military preparedness had deteriorated. National conditions in 1860 convinced many that the town again needed increased protection. The danger now was likely to come not from hostile Indians but their own countrymen.

About 70 men met that May evening. Included were members of some of the town's best known families. Many of their names indicated the strong Mediterranean flavor of the ancient city's inhabitants such as Andreu, Bravo, Bridier, Canova, Colee, Genovar, Llambias, Leonardy, Pacetty, Ponce, and Usina. Three officers were elected for the unit. John Lott Phillips was chosen Captain, Lawrence M. Andreu First Lieutenant, and Charles L. Ridgeley Second Lieutenant. The men chose the name "Florida Independent Blues" for their organization, although they often were referred to as the St. Augustine Blues or, more simply, The Blues.[2]

The Blues' commander, 47-year-old John Lott Phillips, was a prominent citizen and civic official of the town, born on the south Atlantic island of St. Helena on June 15, 1812. Phillips' father had been an officer in the British navy and his mother the daughter of a German major. As

---

David J. Coles is completing work on his Ph.D. degree at Florida State University with a specialty in the American Civil War. His Master's thesis on the Battle of Olustee will be published in the near future.

1. *St. Augustine Examiner*, 19 May 1860. In addition, John Jones, *Florida During the Civil War* (Gainesville: University of Florida Press, 1963) 1-22 provides an overview on the growth of secession sentiment in the state.
2. *St. Augustine Examiner*, 19 May 1860.

a young boy he had frequently visited the exiled Napoleon Bonaparte, recalling later that the deposed emperor was particularly fond of Phillips' ten-year-old sister. Phillips' father eventually resigned his commission, taking his family briefly to Great Britain before settling in the United States. As a young man Phillips served in the Second Seminole War, first as lieutenant and later as captain of a company in the Second Florida Mounted Militia. Future Florida senator David Yulee had apparently served under Phillips' command in this conflict.[3]

After the Seminole War Phillips entered the legal profession, and seemed ubiquitous in the governments of St. Augustine and of St. Johns County. He was elected or appointed to the following offices: Justice of the Peace in 1845, 1847, and 1860, County Auctioneer in 1847 and 1849, Clerk of the Circuit Court in 1857, Judge of Probate in 1859, Notary Public in 1859, and City Council Clerk in the immediate prewar years. In addition, he occasionally acted as captain of the nightly city patrol. Phillips was married and had two sons, John Jr. and Paul, both of who joined the Blues.[4]

The Blues' ranks included other military veterans. Lt. Lawrence M. Andreu had participated in the Battle of Dunlawton in 1836 as a member of the St. Augustine Militia. A number of the company's enlisted personnel had undoubtedly also served in the militia during the Florida Wars.[5]

Little is known of the Blues' activities during the next several months. As a militia unit they were not required by Florida law to perform continuous military duty, but to drill at least once every two months and be prepared for emergencies. Arming and equipping the unit posed a major problem. St. Augustine women probably fashioned uniforms for the men, as women did for other military companies in 1860-1861. At some point a distinctive flag was sewn for the unit. It depicted several cotton balls on a field of royal blue with the inscription "Any Fate But Submission." Today the flag is preserved in the collections of the Confederate Museum in Richmond, Virginia.[6]

3. *Ibid.*; John Lott Phillips Autobiographical Sketch, Ellen Sanchez Phillips Papers, St. Augustine Historical Society Library (hereafter cited as Society Library); Compiled Service Records of Volunteer Soldiers Who Served in Organizations From the State of Florida During the Florida Wars, 1835-1858, National Archives Microcopy M-1086, Reel 25, National Archives, Washington, D. C. A copy of this source is available at the Florida State Archives, Tallahassee, Florida. The reel number is from the FSA copy.

4. "Roster of State and County Officers Commissioned by the Governor of Florida, 1845-1868" (Jacksonville, The Florida Historical Records Survey, 1941), 255-262; Eighth Census of the United States, 1860, National Archives Microcopy M-653, Reel 109, St. Johns County, National Archives; "Patrols" file, St. Augustine City Papers, Society Library.

5. *St. Augustine Examiner*, 19 May 1860, 17 November 1860, 1 December 1860.

6. George Cassel Bittle, "In the Defense of Florida: The Organized Florida Militia from 1821 to 1920" (Ph.D. dissertation, Florida State University, 1965) provides an excellent account of the development of the Florida Militia. Florida Session Laws, 1859 Adjourned Session, 9-11 gives information on the 1859 Militia Laws; Bell Irvin Wiley and Hirst D. Milhollen, *Embattled Confederates: An Illustrated History of Southerners at War* (New York, Bonanza Books, n.d.), 78; Alfred Miller to George Fairbanks, 2 November 1861, Alfred Miller Papers, P. K. Yonge Library of Florida History, University of Florida, Gainesville; Francis P. Fleming, *Memoir of Capt. C. Seton Fleming of the Second Florida Infantry, C. S. A.* (Jacksonville, Times-Union Publishing House, 1884), 26; *St. Augustine Examiner*, 15 June 1861.

On August 25 a group of citizens asked the secretary of war to provide weapons from the local arsenal to arm the Blues. This request was apparently rejected, since on November 10, a public meeting, presided over by John Lott Phillips, asked the state legislature for "the passage of a law authorizing the purchase of suitable number of the most efficient arms of modern warfare, with a view to the thorough arming of the State."[7] During this early period the Blues were probably armed with a variety of obsolete or obsolescent weapons. It is known that several militia companies were later equipped with miscellaneous firearms found in Ft. Marion when it was taken by Florida forces following secession. With the possiblity of war approaching, a military fund of $100,000 was belatedly authorized, and Gov. Madison Starke Perry visited South Carolina to purchase weapons. Despite these efforts, one historian notes that the Florida Militia "ended the year 1860 in an advanced stage of organizational decay."[8]

Lincoln's election on November 6 virtually assured the secession of the lower South. St. Augustine voted overwhelmingly for Southern candidate John C. Breckenridge. Soon after Lincoln's victory, a secession flag was raised over the town and citizens began wearing blue secession cockades.[9]

On Thursday, November 15, militia units from St. Augustine and vicinity met for their annual brigade muster. The *St. Augustine Examiner* noted "the citizen soldiery appeared well, performing the various exercises in a creditable manner."[10] The Blues took part in the muster, and especially impressed the paper:

> This elegant and gallant Corps attracted much attention on Thursday by their soldier-like appearance. The company has for its commander Captain John Lott Phillips, well known as having served with distinction in the Florida War. Such officers and men constitute the best defense of the State in any emergency.[11]

Two days later at a special meeting the company offered themselves to the City Council "to serve as a Patrol to be subject to the Orders of their officers, and independent of the City Patrol's."[12] Concerned over the rapidly deteriorating political situation, the Council gratefully accepted the offer. Lavish in its praise, the *Examiner* called the Blues

---

7. *St. Augustine Examiner*, 17 November 1860; Letter from St. Augustine citizens to the Secretary of War, 25 August 1860, St. Augustine City Papers, Council Minutes, Society Library.
8. Bittle, 222; Johns, 12; William Watson Davis, *The Civil War and Reconstruction in Florida* (1913; Facsimile edition, Gainesville, University of Florida Presses, 1964), 50.
9. Thomas Graham, *The Awakening of St. Augustine: The Anderson Family and the Oldest City, 1821-1924* (St. Augustine, St. Augustine Historical Society, 1978), 89; Johns, 11.
10. *St. Augustine Examiner*, 17 November 1860.
11. *Ibid.*
12. St. Augustine City Council Minutes, 24 November 1860.

"gallant and spirited," and felt that "few finer companies can be found in the Southern States." "The men are all brave fellows, ready to defend their State," the paper continued and, referring to a recent anti-Southern article in a northern newspaper, noted that "If the Editor of the *Chicago Democrat* should come here to make 'the Chivalry eat dirt.' the Blues would like to see him . . ."[13]

Secession sentiment mounted throughout Florida during the final month of 1860. Despite the importance of the Northern tourist trade to St. Augustine's economy, the overwhelming majority of the town seems to have favored disunion. For weeks the *Examiner* ran a boxed heading above its editorial column calling for "The Secession of the State of Florida. The Dissolution of the Union! The Formation of a Southern Confederacy."[14]

On December 20, South Carolina became the first state to leave the Union, followed by Mississippi early in January. As early as November 30, Governor Perry had called for elections to choose delegates to a secession convention, which met in Tallahassee on January 3. Seven days later, by a vote of 62 to seven, this convention took the state out of the union. Even before the secession vote had become final Perry authorized the occupation of the Federal arsenal at Chattahoochee, which was accomplished on January 6. Another obvious target for the insurrectionists was Ft. Marion, valuable for both its psychological importance and its desperately needed cannon.[15]

On January 6, a group of about 25 militiamen from Fernandina arrived at St. Augustine with the intention of removing some of Ft. Marion's armaments for their own use. The following day, almost certainly reinforced by members of the Blues and other militiamen, the troops marched to the St. Francis Barracks and obtained the keys to the fort from the lone army sergeant detailed to guard the installation. Several of Ft. Marion's guns were then loaded on ship and sent to Fernandina.[16]

St. Augustinians learned of Florida's secession on January 12, when citizens brought word of the Tallahassee Convention's action. Immediately church bells pealed in celebration and crowds gathered in the town plaza. The Blues formed in front of a recently erected flagpole, along with Capt. Holmes Steele's Jacksonville Light Infantry. Both com-

---

13. *St. Augustine Examiner*, 1 December 1860.

14. Various issues, *St. Augustine Examiner*, November-December 1860; Graham, 87-90.

15. Johns, 13-22; Davis, 57-68; Dorothy Dodd, ed., "Edmund Ruffin's Account of the Florida Secession Convention, 1861," *Florida Historical Quarterly* 12 (October 1933), 67-76.

16. There is surprisingly little primary material relating to the seizure of Ft. Marion. The only account by a participant is apparently an article by J. Gardner in the 15 July 1914 *St. Augustine Evening Record* entitled "St. Augustine in The War Times." Gardner does not specifically mention the Blues, but it seems highly unlikely that the St. Augustinians would not have participated in the occupation. The official report of the fort's caretaker can be found in *The War of the Rebellion: A Compilation of the Official Records of the Union and Confederate Armies* (Washington, G. P. O. 1880-1901), Series I, Volume I, 332-333 (hereafter cited as ORA). See also Graham, 91-92; Bittle, 243 and Omega G. East, "St. Augustine During the Civil War," *Florida Historical Quarterly* 31 (October 1952), 75-76.

panies appeared "handsomely uniformed and equipped for any emergency."[17] After several speeches a banner handmade by a St. Augustine woman was raised. It was the new national flag of Florida. The *Examiner* recorded the stirring scene as the flag

> "rose beautifully amidst deafening cheers and saluting discharges of artillery and small arms, and as it reached the top of the staff unfolded gracefully and expanded to a favoring breeze, bearing on its ground the cherished Palmetto with an Eagle resting on a globe and holding in its mouth the State's motto, Let us alone.[18]

Within several days the initial burst of jubilation over Florida's secession gave way to a realization of St. Augustine's vulnerability. One inhabitant of the ancient city noted the disappearance of the usually numerous Northern tourists and invalids and the beginnings of an increasingly acute provision shortage. "Those who are not *too poor* to move seem determined to leave . . . I can only say that St. Augustine is far from being a desirable place to live in."[19]

From the time of the occupation of the fort and barracks on January 7 until February 6, the Blues were placed on active state service. Their specific duties during this period are unknown, though they probably patrolled the town and the coast, and strengthened the defenses of Ft. Marion. During this time the building of a redoubt began near the lighthouse on Anastasia Island, and various other defenses were raised at the harbor. On February 7, the provisional government of the Confederacy was formed and Florida's brief life as a sovereign republic ended. The state, wrongly assuming that the Confederacy would now assume the major role of coastal defense, mustered the Blues out of militia service. For the next several months the unit reverted to its earlier duties of occasional meetings and drills. Certainly with the prospect of war mounting, these martial activities assumed greater urgency.[20]

In mid-March an embarrassing incident involving the Blues took place. The City Council, which several months earlier had allowed the unit to conduct its own nightly patrol, revoked the measure. Mayor Rafael Canova commented on the continuing problem of thefts in the community and his belief that the situation was "in a measure attribut-

17. *St. Augustine Examiner*, 19 January 1861.
18. *Ibid.*
19. Benjamin Wright to George R. Fairbanks, 22 January 1861, copy, Fairbanks Papers, P. K. Yonge Library of Florida History.
20. Payroll vouchers for John L. Phillips, Charles Ridgeley, Irvine Drysdale and Lawrence Andreu, in Office of the Comptroller, Territorial and State Military Expenditures, 1839-1869, Record Group 350, Series 43, Box 3, Florida State Archives, Tallahassee, Florida. These records show the period in which the Blues' officers served on active state duty. See also Box 1 for miscellaneous military receipts, a number of which relate to activities in and around St. Augustine. Box 1 also provides information on the various units stationed in the town. Graham, 92-93; East, 75-77; Miller to Fairbanks, 19 January 1861, Miller Papers.

able to the Company called the 'Blues' doing patrol duty under their officers, they failing to make report of their doings to the proper civil authorities." The Council directed that the Blues' patrols be ended, and the militiamen summoned to regular patrol duty as civilians.[21]

The condition of St. Augustine's defenses concerned Governor Perry, particularly following the outbreak of fighting at Ft. Sumter. In late April he asked Adj. Gen. F. L. Dancy to inspect the town and report his findings. Dancy was critical of both the fortifications and the attitude of the inhabitants. He felt only a few guns were needed at the battery near the lighthouse and at Ft. Marion to protect the town. Small detachments of troops at both locations would be sufficient for everyday activities. If an enemy attack was likely, local militia, presumably the Blues, could be called to duty. Dancy then questioned the patriotism of the town's citizens:

> there are not twenty men in the city who would volunteer for distant service. They would all volunteer to occupy the Fort and Eat Rations. They have not forgotten the traditions of the good times under the Spanish Government when they all looked to it for support.[22]

St. Augustinians were outraged at Dancy's report. A meeting at Council Hall chaired by John Lott Phillips called it "Highly injurious to the safety of the city" and formed a committee to report their displeasure to Perry. A petition was sent to the governor in May "Showing our present unprotected state and condition," and asking for additional troops to protect the town.[23] Perhaps this contributed to the decision to again muster the Blues into active State service, which was done on May 24.[24]

St. Augustine citizens must have noticed an increased military activity within the town over the next few months. In addition to the Blues, a portion of the Marion Artillery, the St. Augustine Rifles, and various other units were stationed there. Writing on June 29, resident Alfred Miller commented:

> We still have the troops with us who are very diligently drilled every day in the various sections of our city. The artillery company at the Fort use our front square—the Blues have the Plaza and Capt. L.'s the Barracks ground.[25]

About the first of July the Rifles became the first area unit to leave

21. St. Augustine City Council Minutes, 11 March 1861.
22. Adj. Gen. F. L. Dancy to Gov. Madison S. Perry, 30 April 1861, Fairbanks Papers.
23. St. Augustine City Council Minutes, 18 May 1861.
24. Payroll vouchers, Office of the Comptroller.
25. Miller to Fairbanks, 29 June 1861, Miller Papers.

Troops drawn up in the plaza as shown in *Frank Leslie's Illustrated Newspaper*, December 13, 1862. After the Blues left and St. Augustine was occupied by the United States, Union troops also used the plaza for drilling.

the town for duty in one of the major theaters of the war. The company was ordered to Jacksonville, where the Second Florida Infantry was being formed. Upon leaving, the Rifles were escorted from the town by the town by the Blues and the Marion Artillery, while "quantities of flowers were showered upon the command as they filed through the streets."[26]

The Blues soon followed the Rifles in entering the active Confederate Army. Capt. William Stockton enrolled the unit into Confederate service at Ft. Marion on August 5, 1861. Their initial enlistment was for a period of 12 months, although it was later extended for the duration of the war. The Blues were assigned to the recently-organized Third Florida Infantry as its Company B. This regiment was one of two new units authorized by Pres. Jefferson Davis to help defend the Florida coast.[27]

The Third was a colorful organization composed of companies from many of the counties of eastern and middle Florida. Some, like the Blues, had existed as prewar militia units. Other companies included the Jacksonville Light Infantry, Hernando Guards, Wakulla Guards, Jefferson Beauregards, Duval County Cow Boys, Madison Grey Eagles, Jefferson Rifles, Columbia County Dixie Stars, and the Columbia and Suwannee Guards. The regimental officers were chosen in a election on July 25, 1861. The Colonel was William S. Dilworth, who had originally enlisted as a private in one of the regiment's companies. The unit did not serve together for much of its first year. The majority of the companies toiled on Amelia and Talbot Islands, improving Ft. Clinch and erecting batteries to protect the area. Two companies were posted near

26. Fleming, 27.

27. Compiled Service Records of Confederate Soldiers Who Served in Organizations From the State of Florida, National Archives Microcopy M-251, National Archives, Washington, D. C. (hereafter cited as CSR). Reels 46-52 of this collection consist of the personal service records of the members of the Third Florida Infantry, arranged alphabetically by last name. The number and type of records in each file vary widely, but normally include muster-in papers, by-monthly muster roll abstracts, records of wounds and illnesses, discharge or surrender records, and any other papers relating specifically to the individual soldier. In researching this paper, card abstracts were prepared for each member of the Blues based on information in their files. Additionally, statistical information for the company as a whole was compiled from this source. References to specific files will be listed by name. Those wishing material on an individual soldier should consult his file. The reels are arranged as follows: Reel 46, A-Ca; Reel 47, Ch-F; Reel 48, G-I; Reel 49, J-Me; Reel 50, Mi-Rh; Reel 51, Ri-Sp; Reel 52, St-Z. A copy of this collection is available at the Florida State Archives where it is organized as Record Group 1025, Series 982, Reels 54-60. National Archives Reel 46 contains The Record of Events which consists of abstracts from the regimental and company muster rolls for the Third Florida, including the Blues. It is invaluable for tracing the monthly activities and movements of the unit. Unfortunately, the completeness of the entries vary greatly from month to month and company to company. See also *Soldiers of Florida in the Seminole Indian-Civil-and Spanish American Wars* (Macclenny, Richard J. Ferry, reprint edition, 1983), 99-102; Mrs. R. B. Jarvis, "3rd Florida Regiment—Its Service To The Confederate States," typescript in United Daughters of the Confederacy Scrapbooks, Florida Room, State Library of Florida, Tallahassee. Clement A. Evans, ed., *Confederate Military History: A Library of Confederate States History* (New York, Thomas Yoseloff, reprint edition, 1962) is also an important source. Volume XI of this multi-volume work contains the "Military History of Florida," written by John J. Dickison. It provides important information on the formation of Florida units during the war.

the mouth of the St. Johns River, while the Blues and Capt. David Bird's Jefferson Beauregards garrisoned St. Augustine.[28]

Approximately 79 men had enrolled in the Blues on August 5. A later muster roll showed 99 soldiers in the unit including one captain, three lieutenants, four sergeants, 11 corporals, three musicians, and 77 privates.[29] Additional men joined the company throughout the war. It was a typical Confederate infantry company, with a few notable exceptions. The Blues maintained their militia heritage even on active duty. The very young and relatively old composed a significant percentage of the unit. An amazing 16 of the men were under the age of 17. Oregon Dunham, Paul Phillips, and Rutledge Gould were the youngest at 15. At the opposite end of the spectrum, 14 recruits were over 40. Michael Neligan and James Miller were both 50, while James Gould and Anthony Ponce were senior at age 52. The Confederacy often had to utilize such men, but a newly organized company, particularly early in the war, was not likely to have as many young and old as did the Blues.[30]

The men were volunteers, although several were substitutes procured by more well-to-do St. Augustinians to serve in their place. Andrew Anderson, son of a prominent Unionist family in the town, apparently briefly served in the Blues before hiring Stephen Bennet as a replacement. He eventually left Florida to study medicine in New York until the end of the war. The family of underage Oregon Dunham also found a substitute to serve for him after he was discharged in 1862.[31]

Virtually all the Blues were Floridians, most from St. Augustine. Of the minority with known birthplaces, only Captain Phillips, Brooklyn, New York native James Crosby and Alabama-born Henry Bryan, were born outside the state. As mentioned previously, St. Augustine's Minorcan community joined the Blues in large numbers. Certainly the most unusual, if not unique, aspect of the Blues was the several men of Afri-

28. *Soldiers of Florida*, 99-102; Richard S. Nichols, "Florida's Fighting Rebels: A Military History of Florida's Civil War Troops," (M. A. thesis, Florida State University, 1967), 17-18; ORA I: 1, 470-471 and numerous citations from ORA I: 6.

29. Abstracted from CSR, Reels 46-52; undated muster roll of the Blues, Burt Papers, MC-2, Society Library.

30. Abstracted from CSR, Reels 46-52.

31. *Ibid.* Clarissa Anderson to Andrew Anderson, 25 January 1864, 29 February 1864, Anderson Papers, MC-10, Society Library. Stephen Bennet was probably Stephen A. Benet whose relationship to Brig. Gen. Stephen Vincent Benet is unknown. It is unclear whether Anderson ever formally enrolled in the Blues. There is an Andrew Anderson listed in CSR but this is apparently not the same man. Thomas Graham gives a fascinating account of Anderson's subsequent flight from Florida to New York in his *The Awakening of St. Augustine*, 94-95, and "Letters From a Journey Through the Federal Blockade, 1861-1862," *Florida Historical Quarterly* 55(April 1977), 439-456. Oregon Dunham, Confederate Pension Record D17-233, Confederate Pension Files, Record Group 137, Series 587, Florida State Archives (hereafter cited as Pension records). Dunham attempted to obtain a pension based on the wartime service of his substitute. As with CSR, card abstracts were prepared for each member of the Blues that received a pension from the State of Florida. These files contain a myriad of information, including application forms, approval or denial records, and supporting documentation. Subsequent citations will read Pension Files when referring to general statistical material gathered from these records, and a specific file number if the note applies to a particular soldier.

can or mixed-race ancestry who enlisted. Census and military records show musicians Tony Fontane, Emanuel Osborn, and Isaac Pepino as either black or mulatto. Additionally, one source indicates that another black, Tony Wetters, was a company fifer.[32] Few if any Confederate units had regularly-enlisted Negro members as did the Blues. St. Augustine's Latin heritage, with its less strictly-defined racial distinctions, certainly contributed to this. During the Spanish period slaves regularly joined their masters' units as musicians, but the blacks who enlisted in Company B were apparently free. There is also evidence that another member of Emanuel Osborn's immediate family joined an all-black Union regiment later in the war. It seems unlikely that many other black families could boast veterans on both sides of the conflict.[33]

The occupation and physical characteristics of a number of men are known. Farmers represented the single largest group, with students a close second. The unit also contained two merchants, a gunsmith, house carpenter, painter, sugarmaker, mason, teamster and telegraph operator. The height of the men provides an interesting comparison with that of today. The tallest at 5′10″ were James Allen and John Manucy. Sixteen-year-old Nicholas Andrew stood only 4′10″. It must be noted that these statistics are based on fragmentary evidence available in the service records of some of the men. Unfortunately the files of the majority do not contain such information.[34]

A number of family members enlisted together in the unit. In addition to Captain Phillips and his two sons, William and Alex Middleton were brothers, as were Fatio and Henry Dunham. Undoubtedly other connections existed that are not shown in the official records. For example, among others, surnames such as Ponce, Pacetty, and Leonardy were heavily represented.[35]

The Blues' transformation from militiamen to active-duty Confederate soldiers had no immediate effect on their duties. Throughout the late summer and fall of 1861 they remained at St. Augustine, keeping vigil against a possible Union naval thrust. The arrival of several blockade runners interrupted the monotony, as did numerous false alarms of impending attack. In late September, Alfred Miller noted that the community was "not a little excited" over one such incident and that many

32. Abstracted from CSR, Reels 46-52, particularly files on Fontane, Reel 47, Osborn, Reel 50 and Pepino, Reel 50; Pension records for Tony Fontane, number D14-977, and Emanuel Osborn, number A10-008; Ninth Census of the United States, 1870 gives information on Osborn. Wetters is listed as having served in *Catalog of the Florida Department of the Confederate Museum* (Richmond, Confederate Memorial Literary Society, 1914), 20.

33. "Freedom was as Close as the River: The Blacks of Northeast Florida and the Civil War," paper presented by Dr. Daniel L. Schafer at *Civil War Times in St. Augustine* symposium, April 1986. The exact relationship between the two is unclear.

34. Abstracted from CSR, Reels 46-52 and Pension Files.

35. *Ibid.* Other possible relationships include James and Rutledge Gould, Michael and Henry Neligan, James, Joseph and John Miller and Antonio and John Llambias.

inhabitants kept their belongings packed and ready to leave at a moment's notice.[36]

In November the test firing of a cannon at Ft. Marion led to near panic when residents thought it heralded a Yankee landing. The noise

> startled the whole community . . . the Drums were beating and in a few minutes the long roll was called for all the companys . . . The story was told that a steamer was off the coast but it proved to be only a new feature in their 'tactics'. Nobody was hurt but some lady of delicate nerves came very near it.[37]

Such excitement, however, was rare. Building defenses and drilling occupied most of the men's time. Troops were quartered in the St. Francis Barracks, although a few were probably also housed in Ft. Marion. Illness became a problem during this period. In an effort to improve sanitary conditions, the city ordered that the privy for the Barracks, which was "in a situation offencive to public health" be cleaned and improved.[38]

In December the Blues were briefly transferred to Fernandina, which was believed to be threatened by Northern naval forces. Most of the Third Florida and a number of other units had been stationed there for months, laboring on partially constructed Fort Clinch and nearby batteries. Fernandina was not a particularly healthy or popular location. One member of the Third called it "the meanest place in the S[outhern]. C[onfederacy]." with food so poor it would "give a hog the diarrhoea".[39] Another Confederate was more charitable and described it as "a very pretty place."[40]

It is not known how long the Blues remained at Fernandina. Perhaps they were present in January 1862 when the commander of the Department of South Carolina, Georgia, and Florida, Gen. Robert E. Lee, inspected the post. Within several weeks they were returned to St. Augustine where Captain Phillips was placed in command of the town and the roughly 200-man garrison.[41] The company remained posted there until the evacuation of the town in March.

---

36. Miller to Fairbanks, 21 September 1861, Miller Papers.
37. *Ibid.*, 23 November 1861.
38. St. Augustine City Council Minutes, 14 December 1861; Miller to Fairbanks, 21 September 1861, Miller Papers; Box 1, Office of the Comptroller records.
39. Benjamin Waring Partridge to mother, 13 October 1861, Benjamin Waring Partridge Papers, William R. Perkins Library, Duke University, Durham, North Carolina; CSR, Record of Events.
40. Michael Raysor to wife, 4 August 1861, Michael Raysor Papers, P. K. Yonge Library of Florida History. A detailed account of the Third Florida's activites around Fernandina can be found in Terence H. Nolan's *History of Fort Clinch, Fernandina, Florida* (n. p. Bureau of Historic Sites and Properties, Division of Archives, History and Records Management, Florida Department of State, Miscellaneous Project Report Series #27, 1974), 1-23.
41. CSR, Record of Events; St. Augustine City Council Minutes, 10 February 1862; ORA I: 6, 367-368.

National Archives.

St. Francis Barracks where troops were quartered.

Early 1862 was a dark period for the Confederacy. In February Ulysses Grant won stunning victories at forts Henry and Donelson in Tennessee, and within a short time Nashville was evacuated. Confederate leaders scrambled for troops to defend the rich heartland of the South. Gen. Braxton Bragg called for the abandonment of much of Florida, as did General Lee. Lee felt that the coastal regions should be evacuated, with a few troops concentrated in the interior to repulse raids. Regarding St. Augustine, the general believed the garrison's presence only invited a Union assault. Even before the Northern occupation of the town, the ancient city had in effect been abandoned by the Confederacy.[42]

The day that St. Augustinians had feared and expected for months came on March 9, 1862. That morning an unidentified ship was discovered off the bar at the entrance of the harbor. The ship's appearance created considerable alarm amongst the town's inhabitants. This increased as a small boat was seen taking depth soundings in preparation for entering the harbor. At 10 A. M. Phillips sent a detachment of men to observe these activities from the beach. They returned after several hours with no definite information.[43]

The next day Phillips received orders to "evacuate the place, spike the guns, divide the provisions among the citizens and march immediately to New Smyrna with the Artillery."[44] There would be no fight for the town. At least one person was happy with the decision; Hannah Jenckes wrote a friend on March 10 that "The Blues are ordered to Smyrna this aft. & I hope as much as a pair of pants will not be left behind, if our safety depends on their going."[45]

The Blues left town at 10 P.M. on the evening of March 10. About 30 men accompanied the unit's wagons, while the remainder left in boats. A group of friends and family watched the men depart, no doubt wondering when they would see their loved ones again. Among the Blues who marched away from St. Augustine was 16-year old Bartolo Genovar. His future wife, Mary Louise Gomez who was only ten at the time, watched the troops depart. Later they would be the oldest married couple in the town, with Bartolo surviving to be one of the last Florida Confederate veterans. Two days after the Blues left acting mayor Christobal Bravo, his son a member of the Blues, surrendered St. Augustine to Union naval officer C. R. P. Rogers.[46]

---

42. ORA I: 6, 406; Johns, 61-69; East, 78.
43. East, 78-79; Graham, 99-100; William C. Middleton Diary, 9 March 1862, United Daughters of the Confederacy Scrapbooks, State Library of Florida (hereafter cited as Middleton Diary). This is the typescript of a diary kept by Middleton during much of 1862.
44. Middleton Diary, 10 March 1862.
45. Hannah Jenckes to Mary Martha Reid, 10 March 1862, Samuel A. Swann Collection, Florida Historical Society Library, University of South Florida, Tampa, Florida.
46. *Ibid.;* Middleton Diary, 10 and 12 March 1862; Graham, 99-102. For a Union account of the occupation see the reports in ORA I: 12, 588-602. Biographical file, Genovar, Society Library; Bartolo Genovar Pension record number A08-927.

Fortunately for students of the St. Augustine Blues the typescript of a diary written by unit member William C. Middleton is in the State Library of Florida. It details the unit's activities from the evacuation of St. Augustine through the eve of their first major battle. Middleton recalled that on the evening of March 10-11, the Blues "rowed all night and at dawn the next morning we had reached Matanzas Landing." At Matanzas several last-minute recruits joined the unit. After briefly resting they continued, camping the next night at Dupont's Landing. "Tired and weary, we spread our blankets and under a canopy of stars, in the marsh we slept."[47]

On Wednesday March 12, the men reached Long's Landing, then carried their boats cross-country to Bulow. The St. Augustine garrison had been ordered south to New Smyrna to protect the stores of a recently arrived blockade runner. Before reaching that location however, they learned the supplies had already been unloaded, and headed instead for Volusia, a village on the east bank of the St. Johns River. Over the next six weeks the unit guarded stores and occupied points along the St. Johns and Oklawaha rivers, including Volusia, Hawkinsville, Enterprise, Orange Mills, Welaka, and Orange Springs. In late March, part of the company was ordered to Enterprise to help move munitions, weapons, and supplies from the steamer *Miller*. Included was a quantity of modern Enfield rifles and accouterments, which were used to arm much of the Third Florida. On the 23rd a portion of the regiment defeated a small Union naval force that attempted to land at New Smyrna. The Blues apparently did not participate in this skirmish.[48]

On April 25 the Blues received orders to proceed to Midway, Florida, a hamlet 10 miles west of Tallahassee. The units of the Third Regiment were to rendezvous there, in preparation for being sent out of the state. Arriving on April 30, the troops remained at Midway for 10 days. An unpleasant surprise awaited the men. They learned that the Confederate government had extended the regiment's term of enlistment. No longer was the war expected to last only a matter of months. This decision was met with much opposition, particularly since the officers of some companies had originally promised the men that they would remain in Florida throughout their service. The Blues apparently refused to be mustered in for a period longer than the initial enlistment due to end August 1862.[49]

While at Midway, elections were held for officers to serve throughout the war. One casualty of the reorganization was Lt. Lawrence Andreu, who failed to be reelected to his position. Charles Ridgely was chosen

47. Middleton Diary, 10 March 1862.

48. *Ibid.*, various entries for March and April 1862. See also *Soldiers of Florida*, 100; ORA I: 6, 111-112; CSR, Record of Events for the period of January-April 1862.

49. Middleton Diary, April-May 1862; *Soldiers of Florida*, 100-101; Nichols, 44-46; ORA IV: 1, 1061-1062; CSR, Record of Events.

to replace him. The regiment also received a new battle flag while encamped there, made by a group of Jefferson County women and emblazoned with the motto "We Yield But In Death."[50]

On May 19 the regiment broke camp, having been ordered to reinforce the Confederate army at Corinth, Mississippi. The men marched to Chattahoochee where they boarded a steamer for the trip to Columbus, Georgia. They remained there for one day, before travelling by rail to Montgomery. The Floridians rode into the capitol on May 14, with the mascot of one of their companies, a stuffed wildcat, placed at the head of the locomotive.[51]

The unit never reached Corinth but was instead diverted to Mobile, Alabama. They spent the next two months in and around the city, often standing guard and on provost marshal duty. Several times they received orders to move to various threatened locations, but each was countermanded. Mobile was not a popular place, mainly because of the prevalence of sickness in the area. "Would like to leave here," William Middleton noted on June 30. His brother Alex fell seriously ill with measles, the first of a series of illnesses that hampered him throughout the war, while William suffered from the mumps during this period. Several Blues were discharged for disability at Mobile, and on July 25 Pvt. Thomas Ponce became the first member of the unit to die.[52]

Men discharged from the company faced hardships nearly as great as their comrades on the front lines. As St. Augustine remained under Union occupation, they could not easily return home without the threat of incarceration by Federal troops. For example, due to an illness of the lungs, Domingo Usina was discharged at the conclusion of the 1862 Kentucky campaign. Returning to St. Augustine, Usina asked Union officials for medical aid, but upon his refusal to take an oath of allegiance he was forced to remain in the town on parole. In July 1863 Usina learned that he would be subject to service in the Federal army. He escaped with a companion, stealing a boat and dodging Union pickets until reaching his grandfather's farm north of town. Unfortunately for the fugitives, their hiding place was soon discovered by the Federals and they were returned under arrest to St. Augustine. Usina remained imprisoned for several months when, upon threats of being kept as a hostage for captured Union troops, he reluctantly took a loyalty oath to the United States. "My neck was in jeopardy," he later wrote in explanation.[53]

---

50. *Soldiers of Florida*, 100-101; Abstracted from CSR; Samuel Proctor, ed., *Florida A Hundred Years Ago*, April-May, 1862 (Coral Gables, 1960-1965).
51. *Ibid.*; Middleton Diary, 9-14 May 1862. Middleton enjoyed the unit's brief stay at Montgomery, calling it "a beautiful place, full of hustle and 'lots' of pretty girls." Information on the wildcat mascot is from an autobiographical sketch entitled, "A Short Record of Thomas Benton Ellis, Sr.," P. K. Yonge Library of Florida History.
52. Middleton Diary, 30 June 1862; CSR, particularly Thomas Ponce file, Reel 50. See also John Manucy Pension record number A11-571.
53. Domingo B. Usina Pension record number D14-952.

The families of the Blues also suffered during the war. Union officials exiled from the town many who failed to take the oath of allegiance. Included were a number of relatives of the Blues. Some of them eventually settled in Lake City, which became a haven for expatriated St. Augustinians.[54]

Worried over the fate of their families, many of the Blues were anxious to return to Florida. Despite their concerns the unit remained in Mobile throughout June and most of July. Occasionally unit members were given passes to visit the town at their leisure. Middleton enjoyed speaking with the women of the city but was angered at the high food prices. He also noticed a sign posted in the streets that read, "The Third Florida Regiment, The Indian Fighters Are In Town—Beware Of Them." A proud Middleton recorded in his diary, "No matter what the men say, we have a name and fame with the ladies."[55]

The controversy over the men's enlistment remained a heated issue throughout their stay at Mobile. Their original 12-month term had nearly expired and many of the men had no intention of extending it. Middleton chronicled the efforts to coerce the men into reenlisting:

> Captain Phillips called his company to attention after dress parade and told them that they would receive their pay tomorrow and asked who would reenlist. There was no response.[56]

Two days later the Blues again formed on the parade field. The men "were ordered to step to the front, those slow moving threatened with the guard house." After this, a regimental officer stepped forward and informed the shocked men that they were now officially enlisted for two years of the war. A few of the unfit were discharged at the end of their original term, but the remainder of the company served throughout the war, or until disabled or killed.[57]

The welcome orders to leave Mobile finally arrived on July 20. As the men prepared to break camp, they "were in good spirits, all were glad to leave." Boarding the steamer *R. B. Taney* the next day, the regiment began an uncomfortable, 78-hour voyage up the Alabama River to Montgomery. The vessel "was a large one but hardly large enough to carry one thousand men at one time." Due to the river's low level, several times the troops had to disembark and march along the banks. Hot weather and rain showers added to their discomfort. Tragically, one soldier fell overboard and was presumed drowned. Reaching the Alabama capital on July 24, the regiment boarded trains for Chat-

---

54. Graham, 114-118; "Recollections of E. C. F. Sanchez," *St. Augustine Record,* 30 April 1912.
55. Middleton Diary, 6 June 1862.
56. *Ibid.*, 4 June 1862.
57. *Ibid.*, 6 June 1862; Abstracted from CSR and Pension Files. A large number of men were discharged at the conclusion of the Kentucky campaign in November 1862.

tanooga, Tennessee, where they were to join the army assembling under Gen. Braxton Bragg there. At Chattanooga, the men camped at the foot of Lookout Mountain and waited for the opening of the campaign they knew would soon begin.[58]

The Blues were without their commander as they prepared for battle. Sent to Florida on special orders in late May, Captain Phillips would not return to the company until the conclusion of the upcoming campaign. Eventually promoted to major and appointed regimental paymaster, he remained in service until early 1864, when he was discharged for disability and advanced age. Lieutenant Ridgely assumed command of the company in Phillip's absence.[59]

In the late summer of 1862 generals Braxton Bragg and Edmund Kirby-Smith determined to take the offensive in the western theater. Bragg's original goal was to push Union forces out of middle Tennessee, while Kirby-Smith cooperated with an advance against Cumberland Gap. Ultimately both armies moved deep into the bluegrass of Kentucky. The Third Florida accompanied Bragg's army during the campaign. The regiment suffered through a rude baptism of fire, and was decimated by death, wounds, and illness. Before leaving Chattanooga, Bragg placed the unit in Brig. Gen. John C. Brown's brigade of Maj. Gen. Patton Anderson's division. Other regiments in the brigade included their sister regiment, the First Florida Infantry, the Third Louisiana, and the Forty-first Mississippi.[60]

After some preliminary movements, Brown's brigade marched northward in late August. For the men of the Third Florida, this was their first true taste of campaigning. Long, hard marches exhausted the men, and the mountains they crossed were difficult for the Floridians. After one early advance, William Middleton recalled,

> "It was so hot I threw away part of my clothing. The road all the way was strewn with old clothes, and blankets and sick old men."[61]

Middleton had reason to be despondent as the campaign opened. His brother Alex remained hospitalized in Atlanta, and on August 25 his brother-in-law John Stephens died in a Chattanooga hospital. Middleton briefly left the unit to be with Stephens, reaching him "in time to kneel at his bedside and watch his last breath." After helping bury Stephens

58. Middleton Diary, 20 and 24 July 1862; *Soldiers of Florida*, 101; Jarvis, 3; CSR, Record of Events.
59. Abstracted from CSR and Pension Files. See particularly Phillips and Ridgeley's files, CSR, Reels 50-51.
60. Thomas L. Connelly, *Army of the Heartland: The Army of Tennessee, 1861-1862* (Baton Rouge, Louisiana State University Press, 1967), 187-280 gives perhaps the best summary of the Kentucky campaign from the Confederate viewpoint. See also ORA I: 14, Parts I and II; Kenneth A. Hafendorfer, *Perryville: Battle for Kentucky* (Owensboro, Kentucky, McDowell Publications, 1981); *Soldiers of Florida*, 101; Nichols, 47.
61. Middleton Diary, 21 August 1862.

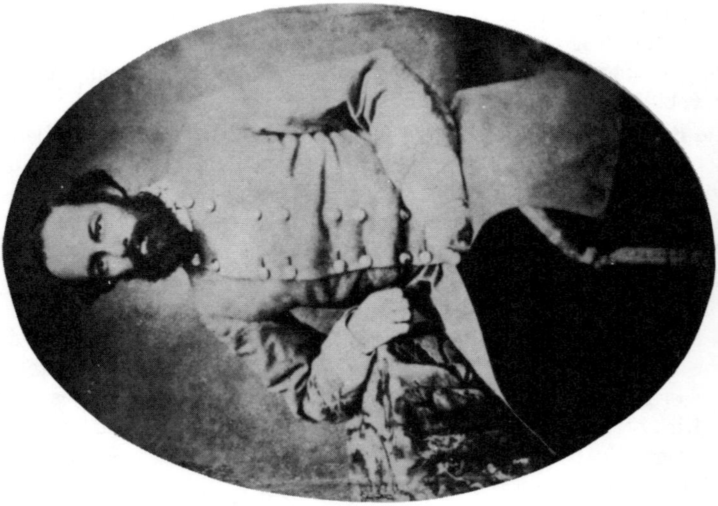

St. Augustine Historical Society.

Gen. Edmund Kirby–Smith, C. S. A.

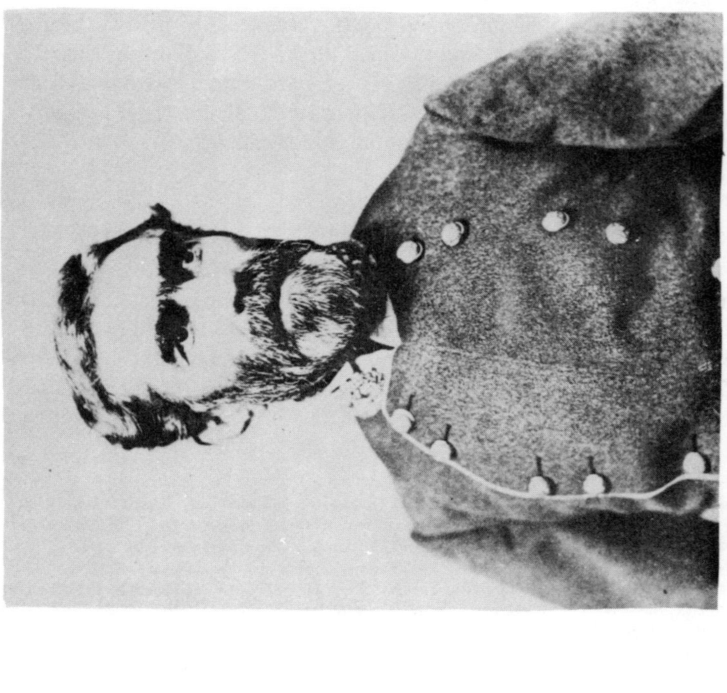

Library of Congress.

Gen. Braxton Bragg, C. S. A.

the next day, "in clean clothes and in a good coffin," Middleton hurried on to rejoin the Blues.[62]

Bragg's army pushed northward into middle Tennessee in early September, crossing parts of the Cumberland Range and Sequatchie Valley. The weather was extremely warm and water scarce. At one point an armed guard had to be placed around a pool of bad water to prevent the nearly thirst-crazed men from drinking. On September 4 Middleton scrawled "nearly perished for water and covered with dust."[63] The march especially taxed the Blues, with the company's large number of old men and young boys. A few of these individuals had been discharged in the previous months, but many more remained with the company. One by one they dropped out along the army's route.

Skirting around Union-occupied Nashville, Bragg moved on toward Kentucky. Marches during this period were particularly brutal. On September 9 and 10 for example, the Blues marched from 3 A.M. to 10 A.M.; rested, then marched from 3 P.M. until 8 P.M. They arose at 2 A.M. and marched through the next evening. Some men fainted from fatigue, others simply fell by the roadside and slept in exhaustion. Others aspects of the campaign were more pleasant. As the Blues passed through towns, young women lined the street, cheering the men and providing news from the front.[64]

The Third Florida forded the Cumberland River on September 10 and crossed the border into Kentucky two days later. Passing through Glasgow, they advanced on Munfordville, where a large Union garrison was isolated and surrounded. On September 13, the Blues captured a Yankee officer they found riding nonchalantly through the countryside in horse and buggy. Two days later at Cave City a number of the unit's sick and broken-down were left in a temporary hospital to recuperate. Unfortunately, Federal forces later captured the location, and the men were taken prisoner and held until eventually paroled.[65]

Brown's brigade hurried on towards Munfordville, the men looking anxiously for their first real combat action.

---

62. *Ibid.*, 25 August 1862, also 1 August 1862; John Stephens (also spelled Stevens) Pension record number A12-508. Following the war, Middleton wrote to the state on behalf of his sister, Stephen's widow, in an attempt to obtain a pension. Stephen's death had left his family destitute. His wife was forced to labor "in the corn and potato field during the balance of the war" to keep her children from starving. See also John Stephens Service file, CSR, Reel 52.

63. Middleton Diary, 4 September 1862, 27 August 1862; abstracted from CSR and Pension Files. One member of the Blues who dropped out during the Kentucky campaign was John A. Steinbeck. During one particularly brutal march Steinbeck fell ill out of the ranks. Lying by the roadside, he was eventually captured and paroled by Union troops. In ragged clothing and with only 25¢ in his pocket, he nevertheless made his way back to Florida. Steinbeck never returned to the Blues. Clarissa Anderson to Andrew Anderson, 26 November 1862, Anderson Papers. Mrs. Anderson also made mention of a number of other members of the Blues that returned to Florida in the fall of 1862.

64. Middleton Diary, 8 September 1862. See also entry for 14 September 1862, A. Oswald Diary, P. K. Yonge Library of Florida History. McDonell, a lieutenant in a Florida unit, commented on the enthusiastic reception received by the Confederates in some areas of Kentucky.

65. Abstracted from CSR; *Soldiers of Florida*, 101; Clarissa Anderson to Andrew Anderson, 26 November 1862, Anderson Papers; Middleton Diary entries for September 1862.

"We were ordered to move to the scene of Action, where we will either gain a victory or fall to the grave, but our trust is in God and we hope for a victory."[66]

The Blues would reach Munfordville too late to participate in the siege. On September 16 the 4000-man garrison surrendered. The Floridians did arrive in time to witness the capitulation, which Middleton described in the last entry of his diary:

"We formed a line on each side of the road and forty-five hundred well dressed well fed Federal Soldiers marched out one by one and gave up their arms—what a contrast to our ragged, foot-sore and weary soldiers who had marched for weeks over mountains and valleys on very short rations."[67]

To Lt. John Inglis of Company D the Unionists "looked fat, clean, & had new uniforms on while we are dirty, ragged, bare-footed and hungry and our skins are black."[68]

Munfordville had been a major victory for the rebels, but it had also slowed their advance and enabled Union Gen. Don Carlos Buell to sidestep Bragg's army and reach Louisville with badly needed reinforcements. The Confederates advanced to Bardstown, but then hesitated, with Bragg unsure of his next movement. The Third Florida reached Bardstown on September 24. On that day a grand review of the army took place. The Blues marched through the town

"With colors unfurled, Bayonets fixed, "Right Shoulder Shift," dressed files, bands in the front, and in fine order and style."[69]

Women lined the streets cheering the troops, while strains of "Dixie", and "The Bonnie Blue Flag" filled the air. One member of the Third recalled "the ladies look[ed] so sweet."[70]

The major battle of the Kentucky campaign occurred on October 8 near the small town of Perryville, about 60 miles southeast of Louisville. On that day a portion of Bragg and Buell's armies met in a unplanned, confused fight. Brown's brigade was detached from Anderson's division

66. Middleton Diary, 15 September 1862.

67. *Ibid.* Middleton apparently completed this entry on 16 September. Unfortunately, this was the last entry made by Middleton in the typescript at the State Library of Florida. He served through the rest of the war, although he suffered from various illnesses, and was often on sick furlough. His brother David never returned to the Blues.

68. John L. Englis Diary, 18-20 September 1862, Special Collections, Robert Manning Strozier Library, Florida State University, Tallahassee, Florida. This interesting diary is a handwritten transcript of a wartime diary kept by Inglis. Entries from this diary have been edited for clarity.

69. *Ibid.*, 24 September 1862.

70. *Ibid.*

early in the battle, and sent to fill a hole on the Confederate right. Lt. Col. Lucius Church commanded the Third Florida in the battle, until he fell wounded and was replaced by Capt. Daniel Bird. The Blues were led by Lieutenant Ridgely, as Captain Phillips had not yet rejoined the unit from detached duty. It is impossible to determine the strength of the Blues as they entered the battle. The previous month's campaign had taken a heavy toll. They probably numbered no more than 40 muskets.[71]

For an untried unit in their first major combat, the Third Florida performed exceptionally. Throughout the long autumn afternoon they were engaged in heavy, seesaw fighting for the possession of two ridgelines. Three times they attempted to break the strong Union lines to their front, and while they did not succeed, they also prevented the Yankees from capturing their position, General Brown fell wounded early in the day, and command of the brigade eventually passed to Col. William Miller of the First Florida. In the Third Regiment Captain Bird was killed in the latter stages of the fight.[72]

The Blues took a large number of casualties. Lieutenant Ridgely was slightly wounded but retained command. More seriously hurt was Lt. Irvine Drysdale, who was hit by a bullet near the left ear. Passing through his head, the missile exited through his left eye. Drysdale survived the ghastly wound, although he would never again serve with the unit. Pvt. Henry Bryan fell dead on the bloody field, as did 23-year-old Alonzo Lopez. At least twelve members of the company were wounded, including Pvt. Francis Weems, who died three weeks later. Many of the wounded fell into Union hands at the close of the battle. Among these was Andrew Beggs, who died in a Danville, Kentucky hospital on October 28.[73]

At one critical moment, the Floridians nearly ran out of ammunition, but the men held their ground, cutting cartridge boxes from their dead and wounded comrades and continuing to fire. Lieutenant Inglis of the Third left a vivid account of the confusion and excitement of the battle:

> The 1st Brigade marched out and Oh Lord. Shells soon came tumbling amongst us. Many knocking men out of their places, wounded several. Rifle firing began in front. . . . we could see for miles in front of us, men getting enough of this, no way to hit back. Soon we saw our line advance and with the wild yells they

71. Abstracted from CSR; *Soldiers of Florida*, 101; Jarvis, 4; Brig. Gen. William Miller, "The Battle of Natural Bridge," 2-4, United Daughters of the Confederacy Papers, Florida State Archives. This typescript includes a detailed account of the brigade's activities at Perryville, written by the man that assumed command of the unit during that battle.

72. *Ibid.*; Hafendorfer, 265, 285-294.

73. Abstracted from CSR and Pension Files. See particularly the Service files of Beggs and Bryan, Reel 46, Drysdale, Reel 47, Lopez, Reel 49 and Weems, Reel 52; Pension record for Drysdale number A11-640.

> cleared the field and crossed the dry creek bed. 'Attention' range along our line; up jumped the 1st Brigade. Gen'l Brown lined us up as if on Drill. Drew his sword and with the command 'Forward, Guide right, March' we started from a march to trot and yelling like the others. We were soon at a run, cut into the brambles, high as our heads, and in terrible bad order. Gen'l Brown stopped to get the Third Fla in line. *Cussed* us from being too quick. 'Dress up or you will be cut to pieces in such order;' the men & officers soon were in line . . .
>
> We again started, and bullets began to whistle, men to fall fast. 'Close up.' . . . We relieved . . . [a] Brigade who cheered us as they moved to the right. . . . We now lay down fire engaging the enemy, firing steady. Gen'l Brown hit, also Col. Church. It hit his shoulder, collarbone broken. The groans of dying & the cries for water of the wounded were terrible. I am nearly killed enemy giving way on all sides. We crawled through the field on our hands & knees. Gen'l Miller in command of Brigade. Came to a fence, pushed it down, and was right at a battery, they are the 10th Ohio. Here it was close to each other . . . we jumped on them, downed them, downed the guns, are chasing the 10th Ohio as they fell back but a few of them left. We had fought and driven them 6 miles. As night came on, we slept right in the line, amongst the dead & wounded[74]

A Perryville historian later wrote of the Floridians: "They had all lived up to the motto of the Third Florida—We Yield But In Death."[75]

Although Perryville ended in a tactical Confederate victory, Bragg determined he could no longer remain in Kentucky and retreated back into Tennessee. By December the Blues were back at Chattanooga, having marched over 700 miles in four months.[76]

The failure of the Kentucky campaign was a severe blow to the Confederacy. Never again would the South mount such an offensive. If this campaign marked a turning point in the war, it also marked the virtual end of the St. Augustine Blues. Few would have recognized the gaunt, pitiful remnant as the same "elegant and gallant corps" that had so impressed the *Examiner* in 1860. When they left St. Augustine in March 1862 the unit numbered between 80 and 100 soldiers. Less than a year later the company entered the Battle of Murfreesboro, Tennessee with only 15 men. After that battle the number was reduced to 10.

---

74. Inglis Diary, 8 October 1862.
75. Hafendorfer, 294.
76. CSR, Record of Events; Hafendorfer, 368-385; Grady McWhiney, *Braxton Bragg and the Confederate Defeat. Volume 1, Field Command* (New York, Columbia University Press, 1969) is the best study of Bragg's baffling generalship.

While many wounded and captured men later rejoined the company, the Blues never regained their former strength.[77]

The Third Florida had been so decimated by its losses in Kentucky that for the remainder of the war the regiment was consolidated with the First Florida. Together the units fought in all the major battles of the western theater. In December 1862 they suffered heavy losses in the bloody, inconclusive Battle of Murfreesboro, Tennessee. The following spring and summer the Floridians marched into Mississippi in an abortive effort to relieve beleaguered Vicksburg. The fall of 1863 brought the blood-letting of Chickamauga and Chattanooga, which opened north Georgia for Union invasion in early 1864. The unsuccessful, four-month campaign to defend Atlanta and Hood's disastrous offensive into Tennessee in late 1864 ensued. The spring of 1865 found the Floridians in the Carolinas, desperately attempting to slow the onslaught of Gen. William T. Sherman's Federal forces. The Blues' long four-year struggle ended on April 26 when Gen. Joseph Johnston surrendered his small army to Sherman near Greensboro, North Carolina.[78]

The remnants of the St. Augustine Blues participated in all these campaigns. Weeded of the unfit and bearing little resemblance to their militia past, the survivors evolved into tough, seasoned veterans. At least 17 Blues died during the war, most of their names inscribed on St. Augustine's monument to its Confederate dead. Scores more were wounded, captured, or discharged for disability. Approximately 120 men served in the unit, but only eight surrendered with the company in 1865. Several more on furlough or detached duty surrendered at other locations. Other, less-complimentary statistics show that at least 10 men deserted the company throughout the war. In early 1863 Andrew Canova, Herbert Pacetty, and Isadore Papy were convicted by court martial and sentenced to six months' hard labor for stealing food from a Tullahoma, Tennessee farmer. Several of the unfortunates imprisoned by Union troops took the drastic step of enlisting in the Northern army to escape the horrors of prison life.[79]

The majority of the company, however, served faithfully until death, disability, or discharge ended their army service. The words of an early historian of the Third Florida provide a fitting, if somewhat overly sentimental, epitaph for the regiment and the Blues as well.

> Had any one told that the Regiment would never see Florida

77. CSR, Record of Events; abstracted from CSR.
78. CSR, Record of Events; *Soldiers of Florida*, 101-102; Jarvis, 4-7; Graham, *Awakening of St. Augustine*, 271.
79. *Ibid.* The figures on the number of men killed, captured, surrendered and deserted should be considered only approximate due to the fragmentary and often contradictory nature of CSR. A rough count shows at least 17 dead, 10-odd wounded, 35 captured and 44 discharged or resigned. Robert Burritt, Ramon Irwin and George Winn all enlisted in the Union army following their capture. See their Service files, CSR, Reels 46, 48 and 52 respectively.

St. Augustine Historical Society.

Confederate War Memorial, the plaza, St. Augustine, ca. 1880.

> again, and that the few who would be so fortunate as to return, would come back after years of toil and suffering he would have been regarded as a prophet of evil. One by one they fell by the wayside. Some lie buried by Georgia's streams, some on the hillsides of Alabama. Some in the valley of Tennessee, some on the bloody fields of Kentucky. Some survived and struggled on till they reached the Carolinas, while a few came back to the old homestead to die in the arms of loved ones. There is many a vacant place in the old Line. Many an unnamed and now sunken mound covers brave hearts who marched, shoulder to shoulder, firm in the resolve to be faithful unto death.[80]

St. Augustine's Confederate sons had not failed in their duty to the nation's oldest city.

80. Jarvis, 7.

Freedom was as Close as the River: The Blacks of Northeast Florida and the Civil War

Daniel L. Schafer

Early in the Civil War, slaveowners in northeast Florida began complaining of slave runaways. These complaints grew increasingly shrill in March and April of 1862, following the permanent occupations of Fernandina and St. Augustine and the temporary seizure of Jacksonville. Although the Federals stayed only briefly in Jacksonville during this first of four occupations, Union gunboats remained on station at Mayport Mills at the mouth of the St. Johns River and regularly patrolled upriver as far as Lake George. These gunboat incursions greatly disrupted commerce on the most important transportation artery in the region; they also barred Confederate fortifications along the shores, provided a measure of protection for Union loyalists and a means of escape for the region's slaves. For the slaves of northeast Florida freedom came to be as close as the St. Johns River. By October 1862 some of these black refugees began joining volunteer Union regiments then training at Beaufort, South Carolina. When they returned to Florida, it was to fight for the Union and to free others from bondage. Until the end of the war slaves from northeast Florida continued to find freedom by escaping to Union forces. Many joined the black regiments of the United States Army and made significant contributions to Union war efforts.

This paper examines the phenomenon of slave runaways in northeast Florida during the Civil War, concentrating on those refugees who fought for freedom in the Union army. It relies on evidence found in contemporary newspapers, personal correspondence and diaries, census data and plantation records where relevant. More importantly, it draws upon the seldom utilized records of the First, Second, and Third South Carolina Volunteer regiments, later mustered into regular service as the 33rd, 34th, and 21st regiments, United States Colored Infantry. More than one thousand slaves from northeast Florida joined these three regiments. The records of their military careers and of their subsequent efforts to obtain pensions provide valuable insights into the lives of black soldiers and the world of slavery in northeast Florida at the time of its demise.[1]

Daniel L. Schafer is professor of history at the University of North Florida in Jacksonville. He is currently chairman of the department.

1. The most useful data on the 1st, 2nd and 3rd South Carolina regiments (subsequently mustered into regular service as the 33rd, 34th and 21st regiments, United States Colored Infantry, hereafter cited as USCI) were Muster Roles and the Regimental Descriptive Books, found in Record Group (hereafter RG) 94 in the National Archives. In addition, when pension records exist for a soldier there is often useful information on his service record, as well as his life before and after the Civil War.

Given the general dearth of evidence, it is difficult to recreate with certainty the response of northeast Florida's black residents to the outbreak of war. Extant newspapers, diaries and personal correspondence written by whites say little on this topic, forcing cautious speculation. An example of this might be seen in the *Southern Confederacy* announcement on February 1, 1861, that Jacksonville's free black community had volunteered to help construct Fort Steele at Mayport Mills. Confidently, the paper reported: "We understand that their patriotic example will be followed by all the other free colored men in this place. What will Messrs. Seward, Greeley, and Co. say to this? Gentlemen, are we not reposing on a mine?" Lacking direct evidence, it is difficult to know why free blacks offered to help construct Confederate defenses, but given their precarious position in a community where secession was seen as a heroic effort to defend the right of slaveholding, and with vigilantes daily stalking the streets, the desire to gain goodwill can not be discounted.[2] In the next few months several of these same free black men volunteered for United States service, joining companies of the First, Second, and Third South Carolina and later returning to Duval County to help dismantle the fortifications at Fort Steele.

With only 31 males between the ages of 14 and 90, Jacksonville's free black population could have made only a small contribution to the work at Fort Steele no matter how willing their participation.[3] Capt. Holmes Steele recognized this, advertising on May 7, 1861, in the *St. Johns Mirror* for "the contribution of slave laborers, for a week or 10 days, for most important work on the fort at the mouth of the river." According to Confederate soldier Willie Bryant there was still plenty of "dirty smutty work going on" at Fort Steele on October 1, when an officer left for Jacksonville with a conscription list intended to raise Negroes to do the heavy labor.[4] No doubt the officer found idle bondsmen to do the work, as the Jacksonville economy was then in a slump caused by the war, which had prompted slaveowners to transfer their laborers from

---

The best primary source on black soldiers is Thomas Wentworth Higginson's *Army Life in a Black Regiment*, Boston, 1870. Dudley Taylor Cornish's *The Sable Arm: Negro Troops in the Union Army, 1861-1865*, New York, 1966, is still the best secondary source. Earlier works which were also helpful are George W. Williams, *A History of the Negro Troops in the War of the Rebellion, 1861-1865*, New York, 1888; Joseph T. Wilson, *The Black Phalanx*, Hartford, Conn., 1980; Luis F. Emilio, *A Brave Black Regiment: History of the Fifty-Fourth Regiment of Massachusetts Volunteer Infantry, 1863-1865*, Boston, 1891; Benjamin Quarles, *The Negro in the Civil War*, Boston, 1953; Bell Irvin Wiley, *Southern Negroes, 1861-1865*, Yale University Press, 1938; Susie King Taylor, *Reminiscences of My Life in Camp*, Boston, 1902; Rupert Sargent Holland, *Letters and Diary of Laura M. Towne: Written from the Sea Islands of South Carolina, 1862-1884*, Cambridge, 1912; William Wells Brown, *The Negro in the American Rebellion; His Heroism and His Fidelity*, Boston, 1867.

2. Richard A. Martin and Daniel L. Schafer, *Jacksonville's Ordeal by Fire: A Civil War History*, Jacksonville, Florida, 1984, chapters 1 and 2.
3. Eighth Census of the United States, 1860, (Washington, 1862), original population schedules, Jacksonville and Duval County.
4. Willie Bryant to Davis Bryant, 30 October 1861, Bryant-Stephens Collection, P. K. Yonge Library of Florida History, University of Florida.

urban to rural occupations or hire them out to work on the Florida Railroad running from Fernandina to the Cedar Keys.[5]

That there was racial hysteria in the air at the time can be judged by the sentences given the slaves implicated in the murder of Mandarin planter Richard Plummer. It is perhaps understandable that the three men convicted of the murder were publicly hanged in Jacksonville on April 26th, but the sentences given to four other men found guilty of complicity were excessive. One man received 160 lashes, two others took 60 strokes, and the fourth suffered 50 cracks of the whip. Considering that prior to the war Florida law permitted only a maximum 39 strokes to prevent crippling or killing a slave, the sentences administered in this case suggest that racial hysteria was responsible.[6]

Beyond occasional newspaper advertisements, there is little direct evidence that slaves were running away in sufficient numbers to raise unusual concern in 1861. In late May, mill owner Samuel Fairbanks expressed frustration concerning the recent loss of Negroes, complaining that soldiers then training near Jacksonville should have been assigned picket detail to end all possibility of escape.[7] Following the November 7 seizure of Port Royal and the increased activity of the Federal blockading squadron off the Florida coast, some planters made arrangements to secure their human chattels by sending them to Georgia. Samuel Fairbanks noted on November 21 that the proximity of the Yankee fleet had prompted several area slaveholders to move their laborers into the interior of the state.[8] By December, whites were becoming less complacent: following his departure from a training camp near Palatka, Captain Winston Stephens of Company B, Second Florida Cavalry, wrote to his wife warning of a possible slave conspiracy. He had heard that six slaves of former Governor Mosely threatened to free themselves if President Abraham Lincoln hadn't accomplished that by January 20, 1862. Stephens was fearful that insurrectionary unrest could spread from Palatka south to Welaka and threaten the safety of his wife and daughter.[9]

Judging from the surviving evidence, however, Stephens' concern appears to have been atypical; most northeast Florida slaveowners were not greatly alarmed at the prospect of losing their chattels via escape, at least not in 1861. All this changed with the arrival of Yankee troops in Florida in March 1862. By this time the slaves of the region had come to see the war as a means to emancipation, and Union forces as vehicles for liberation. Large numbers of slaves abandoned their masters, escap-

5. Andrew Fairbanks to George Fairbanks, 30 August 1860, 4 Feb. 1862, Fairbanks Collection, Special Collections, Strozier Library, Florida State University. See also Martin and Schafer, *Jacksonville's Ordeal*, ch. 2.
6. Samuel Proctor, ed., *Florida A Hundred Years Ago*, April 26, 1861 (Coral Gables, 1960-1965).
7. A. Fairbanks to G. Fairbanks, 24 May 1861.
8. *Ibid.* 21 November 1861.
9. Winston Stephens to Octavia Stephens, 12 December 1861, Bryant-Stephens Collection.

ing both overland and by water to gather as refugees wherever a Yankee military presence could be found.

On February 28, 1862, when Brig. Gen. Horatio G. Wright and his Third Brigade, United States Expeditionary Force, sailed from Port Royal to Fernandina, he carried extensive knowledge of northeast Florida's coastal defenses. For weeks preceeding the departure of the 33-vessel flotilla under command of Flag Officer Samuel Du Pont, escaped slaves and white Union supporters had crossed Union lines with valuable information. Isaac Tatnall, a former slave pilot of the steamer *St. Marys,* proved to be the most effective informant.

When available Confederate troops were ordered to the west by Gen. Robert E. Lee in an effort to stop Union penetration in Kentucky and Tennessee, United States forces captured Fernandina, St. Augustine, and Jacksonville in March while facing only scattered and disorganized resistance.[10] Immediately, runaway slaves began arriving at Union lines. From Fernandina, General Wright wrote on March 10 "Some of these people are left behind, and others are presenting themselves daily, coming in from different directions."[11] From St. Augustine, Lt. J. W. A. Nicholson sent a similar report on the 21st: "Several contrabands have delivered themselves to, or been arrested by, the guard at the entrance to the city. They have fled from their masters who are in rebellion."[12] (Black refugees were called "contrabands of war.")

In Jacksonville the phenomenon of runaways was more dramatic. Under orders to "examine the condition of things in Jacksonville" but to not "occupy any point on the St. Johns River," Lt. Thomas Holdup Stevens was so impressed by the numbers and sincerity of the remaining white Unionist residents that he decided to take possession of the town. General Wright was also persuaded of the wisdom of holding Jacksonville, as was the senior commander, Gen. Thomas W. Sherman, who saw in Jacksonville the germ of a regeneration policy that might one day bring a loyal Florida back into the Union. Flag Officer Du Pont was willing to use naval force to protect the Jacksonville Unionists, even if the 16 companies of army troops were withdrawn. This strong Union presence, coupled with the wide-ranging patrols of the gunboats, galvanized the black slaves of the region into action.[13]

---

10. Brig. Gen. J. H. Trapier to Maj. T. A. Washington, 28 March 1862; Gen. R. E. Lee to Trapier, 34 February 1862, *The War of the Rebellion: A Compilation of the Official Records of the Union and Confederate Armies* (Washington, GPO, 1880-1901), Series I, Volume 6, 93-94, 398-99 (hereafter cited as ORA). See also "Report of S. F. Du Pont." 4 March 1862, *Official Records of the Union and Confederate Navies in the War of the Rebellion* (Washington, GPO, 1894-1927) Series I, Volume 12, 573 (hereafter cited as ORN); *New York Times*, 14 January, 15 March 1862. See also Flag Officer S. F. Du Pont to Capt. J. L. Lardner, 1 March 1862, Du Pont to Comdr. P. Drayton March 2, 1862, Du Pont to Secty of the Navy Gideon Welles, 1 March 1862, ORN I: 12, 572-575; Brig. Gen. H. G. Wright to Du Pont, 5 March 1862, Lt. T. H. Stevens to Du Pont, 7 March 1862, ORN I: 12, 581-585.
11. Brig. Gen. H. G. Wright to Capt. Louis H. Pelouze, 10 March 1862, ORA I: 6, 143-4.
12. Report of Lt. J. W. A. Nicholson, 21 March 1862, ORN I: 12, 643.
13. Du Pont to Stevens, 7 March 1862, ORN I: 12, 586-7; Gen. T. W. Sherman to Adj. Gen. L. Thomas, 16 March, 25 March 1862, ORA I: 6, 248-50; *New York Times*, 20, 24, 26, 31 March, 2 April 1862; Calvin

Anticipating the arrival of Union forces, Samuel Fairbanks took his Negroes upriver and left them at a Clay County location on Doctors Lake. He then returned down river until gunboats appeared and he sought shelter with a friendly planter. After a discreet delay Fairbank's slaves John and Frank, an engineer and a laborer at the Fairbanks' mill, stole a boat and paddled back to Jacksonville. By the time Fairbanks tracked them down, they had grown accustomed enough to freedom to refuse his order to return to Clay County. Obtaining the cooperation of Jacksonville's still functioning civil authorities—many of the remaining Unionists were slaveowners—Fairbanks had Frank jailed for his "saucy" behavior. Later, however, the jail was broken open and Frank escaped to Fernandina. John, along with another Fairbanks slave named Charlotte, escaped to Mayport Mills, but Fairbanks soon persuaded Union officers to return the couple to his custody. Before he could locate a boat to carry the couple back to Doctors Lake, however, the Union command decided to leave Jacksonville and to carry loyal residents, as well as some contrabands including John and Charlotte to safety at Fernandina and Hilton Head.[14]

When the first Union occupation ended on April 8, Fairbanks had lost nine slaves, although two were subsequently returned. John and Frank volunteered for Union service in Company A, First South Carolina Volunteer Infantry. When Fairbanks heard in July 1863 that John, "our [former] engineer," had been shot that summer, he wished the same fate for Frank. By the end of the war Frank also was dead.[15]

Friends of Fairbanks suffered even heavier losses to the invading Yankees. In one escape, 23 men and women from three neighboring plantations fled together, pursued by an armed vigilante posse. One escapee, an elderly and hitherto loyal servant known as Old Banjo, was shot in the head and killed by the vigilantes.[16]

Joseph Cryer and his son Andrew escaped to Union lines from the Diego (Palm Valley area) plantation of Jacob Mickler. For James and Henry Adams the route to freedom was a trip across the St. Johns River; the brothers were the property of Francis Richard in the Empire Point vicinity. Andrew Murray, a native of St. Augustine, was the property of Joseph Finegan when he escaped to Fernandina soon after hearing rumors of Federal forces there. Thomas Long, the slave of John R. Roberts, and Charles McQueen, the slave of a Mr. Eubanks, also made their way to Jacksonville and were aboard the Union transports when the city was evacuated on April 9, 1862. In October and November of

Robertson, "An Account of Some of My Experiences," undated typescript, p. 29, Jacksonville Historical Society Library; John Daniel Hayes, ed., *Samuel Francis Du Pont, A Selection From His Civil War Letters*, (Ithaca, Cornell University Press, 1969) I: 373; Martin and Schafer, ch. 3.

14. S. Fairbanks to G. Fairbanks, 21, 29 April 1862.
15. *Ibid.*, 10 May 1862, 4 July 1863. See also Muster and Descriptive Books, Co. G, 33rd USCI.
16. W. Stephens to O. Stephens, 23 October 1862.

1862, each of these men volunteered for military service in the First South Carolina.[17]

The free black population of northeast Florida also sought protection behind Federal lines in March and April 1862, several volunteering later for Union military service. Benjamin Williams was living in Jacksonville in 1860, listed in the census of that year as having been born in the free state of Maine. Alonzo H. Phillips, born in Jacksonville, became a commissary sergeant in Company A, Third South Carolina. Henry Hannahan, born free in 1833 at Pablo Beach, became a sergeant-major of the same company. Lewis Forester, born a slave but freed as a boy when purchased by his father, escaped to Fernandina in 1862. He volunteered for service in Company A, Third South Carolina in June 1863. His brother George Forester, also a free man, joined the United States Navy in 1862, as did Henry Johnson and James P. Lang. Other Duval County free blacks who can be identified as joining the black South Carolina regiments are Albert Sammis, George Floyd, Frank and Alexander Hagen, John Lacurgas, Charles Lang, Levi and William H. McQueen, Samuel Petty, John B. Richard, Walter Taylor, James Simmons, Henry and James Williams.[18]

Union volunteers from St. Augustine in Company D, First South Carolina, included Samuel Osborn and his son Samuel Jr., free colored residents since at least 1850. It is an unusual occurrence that another Osborn son, Emmanuel, volunteered for the St. Johns Grays, a Confederate militia company formed in St. Augustine. It appears that free colored families were not immune to the tragic and often-discussed situation where white families were divided by their Civil War loyalties.[19]

Abraham Lancaster enlisted in Company F, First South Carolina in 1863. Other free colored from St. Augustine that can be followed into the Union regiments are Pablo Rogers, James Lang, James Hills, James

---

17. Many of the men identified here as free before 1861 were listed in one or more census from 1830-1860 for Duval, Nassau and St. Johns counties. These were often incomplete, however, and I have tentatively traced a few black soldiers to families of the same name who listed sons with corresponding ages in one or more census. The Regimental Muster and Descriptive Books, RG 94, sometimes identify volunteers as free blacks at the time of muster-in. Union pension files also identify other men who were free prior to 1861, generally through the depositions taken by the various investigators. Because the men faced great difficulties in proving their eligibility and worthiness after applying for pensions, it was not unusual for fifteen to twenty USCI veterans to testify on behalf of their wartime comrades. Pension records in the National Archives contain information about northeast Florida that is not available elsewhere. Pension records used here are those for Joseph Cryer, number 452.263; James Adams, 254.507; Henry Adams, 874.759; Andrew Murray, 689.587; Thomas Long, 1.125.870; Charles McQueen, 343.261, RG 15, Records of Veterans Administration, National Archives.
18. *Ibid.*, Alonzo H. Phillips, 839.924; Henry Hannahan, 721.857; Lewis Forester, 808.976 and 288.415.
19. Pension records for the two Samuel Osborn's are 998.33, 778.686, and 998.312. The family is listed in the 1850 Census of St. Augustine under the name Ausbourn, and includes Samuel, age 41, Marisa 53, Alex 12, Manuel 8, Sam 6, and Elisabeth 2. The 1860 Census spells the name as Osburn and lists Samuel as age 40, Maria 55, Manuel 14, Samuel 12, and Elizabeth 10. Perhaps the Osborn family found the elusive St. Augustine Fountain of Youth.

Ash, George Garvin, William Morris, Alexander Clark, and the Pappy brothers, Antony, Frank and William.[20]

By the time the Jacksonville evacuation fleet reached Fernandina in April 1862, the exodus of black laborers from northeast Florida had reached alarming proportions. Slaveowners were terribly disturbed by this exodus and fearful that their crops would go unharvested, but were not yet willing to believe that their slaves had been permanently freed. Encouraged by several instances when Union officers at Jacksonville and Mayport had returned escapees to their owners, Fairbanks and Stephen Bryan travelled to Fernandina in an attempt to reclaim their lost bondsmen. When an "abolitionist Lt. Colonel" refused an interview, Fairbanks complained that General Wright had in Jacksonville "afforded every facility for masters to claim and take away their negroes and every day they were claimed and taken away by their owners. The naval officers also [did] the same, towing boats up the river with them."[21] Ironically, Fairbanks and Bryan carried with them a letter from Lieutenant Stevens in Jacksonville praising them as "gentlemen of character and influence" and requesting Union officers in Fernandina "to give them whatever facilities your official position may afford toward securing the objective of their mission."[22] The rejection was puzzling to Fairbanks, especially when contrasted with the return of two of his slaves, Jim and Sally, who had been aboard a Union vessel that steamed back to Jacksonville March 10 under flag of truce to return fifty-two slaves to their owners.

Before July 1862 Union policy concerning human contrabands of war had been inconsistent, depending often on either the pro-abolition or the pro-slavery sentiments of the officers in charge. Logs of the gunboats patrolling the St. Johns River document that black refugees were routinely judged to be the property of Confederates and, therefore, were not returned to their owners. On April 1 and 2, 1862, for example, the *Seneca* picked up eleven contrabands on the St. Johns River and carried them to freedom at Hilton Head.[23] General Wright followed the common practice of cooperating with slaveowners who remained behind Federal lines and were presumed to be loyal Unionists. Rebel slaveholders were not accorded these privileges and requests to remove contrabands to enemy lines were refused.[24] Lieutenant Stevens appears to have followed Wright's policy, but tended to extreme cooperation with slaveowners, especially since affiliation often depended upon who was in control of the region, and control fluctuated often from 1862 to 1864.

20. *Ibid.*, William Pappy, 363.496; Thomas Long, 1.125.870; James Lang, 1.166.518.
21. S. Fairbanks to G. Fairbanks, 21 April 1862.
22. Stevens to Drayton, 3 April 1862, ORN I: 12, 705.
23. Logbook of the *Seneca*, Daniel Ammen, Lieutenant Commanding. Select List of U. S. Navy Logbooks, Record Group 24, National Archives. See also Logbooks for the *Ottawa* and *Water Witch* under various commanders.
24. Report of Brig. Gen. H. G. Wright, 13 April 1862, ORA I: 6, 124-5

Wright's action in returning fifty-two slaves to Confederate command at Jacksonville, leaving them at the dock to await reclaiming by their owners, went far enough beyond cooperation with Unionist slaveowners to constitute an indirect benefit to Confederate forces. During the evacuation, which saw all the Union supporters leave, Wright ordered all runaway slaves off the vessels to be reclaimed by their owners. Wright's own men refused to cooperate, however, smuggling many contrabands back aboard the ships, only to have them returned upon reaching Fernandina.[25]

By late April bands of vigilantes had become the scourge of the countryside, wreaking violence on Unionists and Negroes suspected of pro-Union activites. One man called himself "a Guerilla in every sense of the word" and boasted: "We have made some arrests, both black and white, and hung one negro . . . last week. . . . We have three men spotted that ought to be hung."[26] It was partly because of this violence that Du Pont ordered on July 3, 1862 that naval personnel stop returning contrabands to their owners. Du Pont had also been influenced by reports which described the vital link between slave laborers and Confederate food supplies. One writer said of the St. Johns River valley: "the whole of the banks of the river as far as one can see is planted with corn. They say corn enough is in Florida for all of the Southern rebel States. If we carry their darkies off they can not gather it."[27] After Du Pont made his decision, even Unionist slaveowners were told to submit claims to the government, but that restoration of slave property would await the conclusion of the war.

Anxious to test the resolve of Union officials on contraband policies, Samuel Fairbanks, Stephen Bryan, and other Jacksonville slaveowners sent Judge Samuel Burritt to Hilton Head in late April to confer with Gen. David Hunter, hoping to obtain the return of recent slave runaways. Hunter, an avowed abolitionist, was not encouraging. The audacious Burritt continued on to Washington where he arranged a meeting with President Lincoln. According to Samuel Fairbanks' version of the meeting, Lincoln was at this point still a reluctant emancipator, prompted by the threat of border state disaffection. Fairbanks wrote: "Lincoln could not commit himself but Burritt says that he thinks Lincoln is not an abolitionist and that the negroes will be returned at the end of the war."[28]

Despite the inconsistency in Union policy slaves from northeast Florida continued to run away in numbers alarming to their owners even after the evacuation of Jacksonville in April 1862. Union gunboats continued to patrol the St. Johns and some of its tributaries, stopping often

25. Col. W. S. Dilworth to Captain T. A. Washington, ORA I: 6, 131.
26. J. W. Pearson to Gen. Richard Floyd, 8 April 1862, ORA I: 13, 233.
27. Nicholson to Du Pont, 17 June, 3 July 1862, ORN I: 13, 110, 167.
28. S. Fairbanks to G. Fairbanks, 10 July 1862.

to take aboard black and white refugees. Late in May, a gunboat anchored off Stephen Bryan's plantation. Fairbanks reported that "twenty-four of his negroes escaped and took refuge on [the gunboat]."[29] The next day Bryan drove the remainder of his slaves, along with 67 chattels of his two closest neighbors, to unoccupied land in the interior of the state. That meant, Fairbanks predicted, that 15,000 to 20,000 bushels of corn in east Florida might go unharvested for lack of labor. Confederate cavalry officer Winston Stephens, encamped outside Jacksonville at the time, echoed Fairbanks' concerns, predicting "they will not be able to save their crops."[30] Although Stephens was able to capture near his camp on the river two contrabands from Ocala who were trying to get to the gunboats, he estimated in July 1862 that 1,500 black refugees had already gathered in Fernandina.

In August, Fairbanks lamented: "Negroes are gradually getting away—singley and by two's and threes—the coast is pretty near drained."[31] Regimental records of the South Carolina Volunteers give credence to Fairbanks' comments. One of the singles escaping in July was David Flemming. Flemming escaped July 10, 1862, making it safely to Mayport, where he found freedom on a Union gunboat. On November 11, 1862, he enlisted in Company G, First South Carolina.[32]

From the St. Johns a planter's daughter wrote to Ellen Call Long in Tallahassee saying her father had decided it was "impossible to keep negroes on the river now." Soon after the Yankees arrived on the river her father had "discovered our servants about to bid farewell to the place; so next morning he packed them all off to the interior. Can you imagine how we got along without a single servant? . . . father determined it was better to have a home without servants than servants without a home. So we stay here living on cornbread and hope, our only consolation that we are no worse off than our neighbors."[33]

That planter and Samuel Fairbanks could no doubt have sympathized with the anguish of a former St. Augustine merchant who lost 15 slaves in Key West to the Union contraband policy. Writing to his son Henry to explain what this loss meant, Christian Boye explained:

> My dear son, those slaves of mine were worth to me a year ago, seventeen thousand dollars and there was some 10 young ones among them who increased in value every day.
>
> My yearly income from them was not less than from $2000.00 to $2500.00. I could afford to send you and your sister to expensive schools. You will see, as this income is stopped, and God knows

29. *Ibid.*
30. W. Stephens to O. Stephens, 24 July 1862.
31. S. Fairbanks to G. Fairbanks, 12 August 1862.
32. David Flemming, pension record 273. 637.
33. Ellen Call Long, *Florida Breezes*, (Gainesville, University of Florida Press, 1962), 331.

> when it will begin again. I am obliged to use strictest economy, turn a penny a dozen times before I spend it. The loss of our slaves forces me to take Mary from school next Spring if not sooner—as I cannot make enough to pay her school bills.[34]

Boye warned his son to stay away from Key West. Since the arrival of the Yankees, Boye said, it had become only a place "to learn bad habits."

Another man who could sympathize with Boye was the Confederate Gen. Joseph Finegan. For years a northeast Florida slaveowner, and one who had lost laborers to the Union gunboats, Finegan understood the importance of slavery to Florida's economy and was willing to tailor Confederate strategy to protect that vital connection. In May 1862 Finegan began moving men and artillery to the lower St. Johns in an effort to stop the Union gunboat incursions. By September 4 he was ready to gamble, sending Winston Stephens' cavalry company on a diversionary raid on Mayport to tie up the gunboats so cannons could be mounted on the east bank of the river at St. Johns Bluff, and on the west bank at Yellow Bluff, the two highest points near the river's entrance. If the Confederates were able to deny access to the gunboats, Finegan reasoned, freedom would no longer be as close as the St. Johns River. The route of escape would be forced overland through rebel security and civilian patrols.[35]

Following a series of artillery exchanges that stopped the gunboats below St. Johns Bluff, Samuel Fairbanks was ecstatic in his praise of Finegan's actions. At last, he wrote, the gunboats had been stopped. Had this action been taken sooner, Jacksonville would never have fallen to the Yankees in March and the slaves would never have escaped, Fairbanks proclaimed. He did, however, "hope that the negroes will go along without too much trouble. . . ."[36]

Finegan's measures proved only a temporary respite. On October 1, 1862, as gunboats bombarded the Confederate gun installations, Yankee troops landed along the Pablo River and marched toward St. Johns Bluff from the land side. They were led by a man described as "Israel, our faithful Negro guide who ran away from Jacksonville a few weeks since and is thoroughly acquainted with all the country."[37] The bluff was hastily abandoned while rebel troops retreated towards the interior. Union forces continued upriver to occupy Jacksonville for a second time on October 5. While Finegan worked feverishly to regroup his demoralized troops and establish lines west of the town, slaves in the

---

34. Christian Boye to son, 23 September 1862, Typescript, Biographical File, Boye, St. Augustine Historical Society Library.
35. The story of St. Johns Bluff and the second occupation of Jacksonville is told in Martin and Schafer, 100-117. The key accounts are Brig. Gen. John M. Brannan to Gen. O. M. Mitchell, 4 October 1862, and Col. C. F. Hopkins to Gen. Joseph Finegan, 8 October 1862, ORA I: 14, 127-32, 138-41.
36. S. Fairbanks to G. Fairbanks, 24 September 1862.
37. Valentine Chambers to friend, 10 October 1862, MS Box 7, P. K. Yonge Library.

From ***Confederate Military History,***
Volume XI, Florida by J. J. Dickison

Gen. Joseph Finegan, C. S. A.

region realized that the chaotic conditions again favored escapes to freedom.

As the slaves of A. M. Reed discovered, however, individual vigilance by the planters was still operational. At Reed's Mulberry Grove plantation south of Jacksonville, a mass runaway attempt was thwarted when the conspirators were discovered by a white neighbor. As Winston Stephens described the event: "All of Mr. Reads [sic] negroes had packed up to go off at night and they were seen by [Peyre] Pearson and he ordered one of the men to stop and he then got Mr. Reed up and he went in the kitchen and there everthing was ready and Perry attempted to run off and he was shot in the legs and I think they are sent off to be sold. long legged [sic] Jake got to the Gunboat and the Yankees went back with him after his family but they had moved out in the country and Jake made a terrible fuss."[38]

A. M. Reed recorded the same event in his diary, writing tersely: "About 12 p.m. [Oct. 5] found my negroes preparing to leave. In the melee, Jake and Dave ecaped carrying off my boat, the Laura Shaw."[39] Forewarned of the danger to his other slave properties, Reed acted swiftly. His diary entry for October 6 states: "Started all the negroes . . . for the interior."

Reed must have been astonished on October 7 when Jake returned. He wrote, "U. S. Gunboat, Patroon, stopped at my wharf. Sent up Lieutenant Potts of the flagship, [and] Captain Steadman, with a file of men bringing the runaway, Jake, to get his family and things."[40] Learning that his wife Etta had been sent into the interior, Jake could only remonstrate and return to Jacksonville aboard the *Patroon*. When the town was evacuated three days later he was among the 276 contrabands carried away by the navy transports.[41] But A. M. Reed had not seen the last of Jake.

Samuel Fairbanks wrote of the second Yankee occupation of Jacksonville: "They shall probably steal what few negroes there are left and destroy at will."[42] Fairbanks was furious to learn that the Federals had destroyed a thousand boats along the St. Johns but after reconsideration welcomed the act, saying that at least it would keep the Negroes from rowing to the gunboats.

One group of enterprising contrabands found it possible to gain freedom without small boats. Lt. S. S. Snell and a small naval force worked in the Palatka area for two days in mid-October, raising two barges sunk by the rebels. As soon as the barges were floated successfully, 49

38. W. Stephens to O. Stephens, 4 November 1862. See also S. Fairbanks to G. Fairbanks, 7 October 1862.
39. "The Diary of A. M. Reed, 1848-99," (copy prepared by the Historic Records Survey, Works Progress Administration), William R. Perkins Library, Duke University.
40. *Ibid.*
41. Brannan to Col. W. P. Prentice, 13 October, 1862, ORA I: 14, 131.
42. S. Fairbanks to G. Fairbanks, 6 October 1862.

contrabands appeared on the shore, boarded the barges and were towed down the river to Mayport.[43]

Mass runaway attempts appear to have been atypical in October 1862, perhaps because of increased surveillance following the runaway problems of previous months. Most contrabands escaped alone or with their families. James Bagley, James Bagley, Jr., Henry Harrison, Jackson Long, Lewis McQueen, Benjamin Turner and Thomas Holzendorf joined various companies in the South Carolina regiments in 1862. The last named escaped with his wife, Harriet and two children, who followed Holzendorf to regimental camps throughout the war.[44]

Union troops stayed in Jacksonville less than a week during the second occupation, leaving on October 11, 1862. Looking back from the deck when the Federals evacuated were Jake Reed and 275 other contrabands. Numerous other escapees had previously been carried to Mayport and Fernandina. After the evacuation Winston Stephens complained that the Yankees stole and vandalized, acting "more like black hearted scamps in Jacksonville than they ever have on the river."[45] Finegan's terse report on the evacuation emphasized the loss of black laborers. The Yankees he said, "have taken all the negroes, free and slave, they could find in the place."[46] General Finegan ordered Capt. J. J. Dickison to round up all Negroes—free or slave—and to remove them "from the St. Johns River into the interior at a safe distance from the enemy." Winston Stephens reported that several Negroes had been shot in Jacksonville in mid-October, and that others were being harrassed by Confederate cavalry. Samuel Fairbanks concluded that slave property was no longer safe on the St. Johns; in early December he took his remaining two slaves to Georgia to be sold as other planters did at this time.[47]

While Finegan and his Confederate command struggled to reassert control, contrabands flocked into Union-occupied Fernandina, St. Augustine, and Key West. Many found their way to Beaufort, South Carolina, where Union officers had been attempting since May 1862 to organize an experimental phalanx of black soldiers, recruited from the swelling ranks of refugees. The first regiment, unsuccessful, had been

43. S. S. Snell to Charles Steedman, 14 October 1862, Steedman Collection, MS Box 27, P. K. Yonge Library. That not all Union officers reacted favorably to blacks in the Union army can be seen by Steedman's 20 March 1863 letter to his wife. In response to his gunboat, *John Paul Jones*, being sent to Jacksonville to protect army units, he said: "The duty has been by no means to my taste as the army force was composed entirely of niggers."

44. Muster and Descriptive Books, 33rd and 34th regiments of USCI, RG 94. See also Thomas Holzendorf, pension record 752.605.

45. W. Stephens to O. Stephens, 4 November 1862. See also 15, 23 October 1862, and Finegan to Gen. S. Cooper, 9 October 1862, ORA I: 14, 633, 661.

46. Finegan to Cooper, 9 Oct 1862, ORA I: 14, 633.

47. W. Stephens to O. Stephens, 15 October 1862; D. Bryant to W. Bryant, 21 December 1862. See W. Stephens to O. Stephens, 4 November 1862. See also ORA I: 14, 661.

disbanded in August. Only a single company was retained for unofficial garrison duty at Saint Simon Island.[48]

On August 25, 1862, Secretary of War Edwin M. Stanton, prompted by a shortage of men for operations in the South, issued orders to Gen. Rufus Saxton to arm and equip up to five thousand "volunteers of African descent." Inheriting only the one company from the earlier regiment, Saxton set to work in earnest to fill the ranks of the First South Carolina Volunteers. By November 3, 1862 he was ready to test the black men's courage and utility, sending Company A on a destructive raid on the Florida and Georgia coast. Saxton described the expedition as a "perfect success. . . . The negroes fought with a coolness and bravery that would have done credit to veteran soldiers. . . . They seemed like men who were fighting to vindicate their manhood and they did it well."[49] The commander of the raid reported that his men "behaved bravely, gloriously, and deserve all praise." Lt. Col. Oliver Beard said, "I started from Saint Simon's with 62 colored fighting men and returned to Beaufort with 156 fighting men (all colored). As soon as we took a slave from his claimant we placed a musket in his hand and he began to fight for the freedom of others."[50]

General Saxton saw in the expedition the germ of a larger war policy, one that could cripple plantation production and force the Confederate command to divert manpower from Northern battlefields. Calling the raid "one of the important events of the war—one that will carry terror to the hearts of the rebels," Saxton proposed to arm and barricade a number of light-draught vessels, each manned by 100 black soldiers, to run up the coastal rivers and capture plantations. Expecting hundreds of slaves to flock to the gunboat whistles, Saxton could "see no limit to which our successes might not be pushed up to the entire occupation of states. . . ."[51]

Lieutenant Colonel Beard led his black troops on another Georgia coastal raid on November 13, but further application of Saxton's plan was delayed by the arrival of a new regimental commander. The man chosen to lead the first black regiment was Thomas Wentworth Higginson, a captain in the 51st Massachusetts Regiment. Sensing that a dramatic chapter in the history of the nation was about to be written, Higginson accepted the position immediately, saying: "I had been an abolitionist too long, and had known and loved John Brown too well, not to feel a thrill of joy at last on finding myself in the position where he only wished to be."[52]

---

48. See the 20 January to 13 March 1862 letters of Gen. T. W. Sherman and Wright in ORA I: 6, 219-45.
49. Saxton to Stanton, 12 November 1862, ORA: 14, 189-92.
50. *Ibid.*, Beard to Saxton, 10 November 1862.
51. *Ibid.*, Saxton to Stanton, 12 November 1862.
52. Howard N. Meyer, "Introduction," in Thomas Wentworth Higginson, *Army Life in a Black Regiment* (New York, Collier Books, 1962), 7-23, 29.

A stickler for drill and discipline, Higginson put his troops through a rigorous training schedule stressing order and regular military discipline. Although military goals and training took priority, Higginson still stressed abolitionist ideals; he routinely told the recruits: "You are fighting for your own liberty and the liberty of your children. Nobody can make you free unless you have the courage to fight for your own freedom. And if you resolve to be free nobody can make you slaves."[53]

In his diary on December 2, 1862, he recorded, "Today General Saxton has returned from Fernandina with seventy-six recruits, and the eagerness of the captains to secure them was a sight to see." The following day he commented on a special company of "all Florida Men." Higginson thought them to be: "the finest-looking company I ever saw, white or black; they range admirably in size, have remarkable erectness and ease of carriage, and really march splendidly. Not a visitor but notices them; yet they have been under drill only a fortnight, and a part only two days."[54]

Higginson probably referred to Company G, a unit in which over one-half the recruits listed Florida as their state of birth. Of the 106 mustered into Company G, 57 gave Florida as their birth place, while 25 of that number said they were born in either Jacksonville or Duval County, and 27 listed St. Augustine, Fernandina, Palatka, or other northeast Florida locations. In the final count, in excess of 450 volunteers in the First, Second and Third South Carolina regiments gave northeast Florida as their place of birth.[55]

In all the companies of the three South Carolina regiments the influence of the Florida men is inescapable. Samples from the regimental muster rolls indicate that in the three South Carolina regiments alone there were more than 1,000 volunteers that came from Northeast Florida plantations and towns. Considering that the 1860 Census listed 11,756 slaves for Duval, Nassau, and St. Johns counties (the total includes adult men and women as well as children), and that many owners either sold their chattels or moved them to secure locations in the interior of the state prior to the arrival of Union troops, the 1000 volunteers represent a significant percentage of the adult male slaves living in the region in 1862.[56]

The backgrounds for these northeast Florida volunteers were surprisingly diverse. Based on a sample of 364 recruits from the region, the median age was 24, yet 42 gave their ages at the time of muster as 40 through 60. The majority of the recruits, 65 percent, were engaged

53. Higginson to Co. G, 25 November 1863, General Orders No. 1, Order Books, 33rd Regiment USCI, RG 94.

54. Higginson, 42.

55. Muster and Descriptive Books, 33rd, 34th, 21st regiments, USCI, RG 94.

56. The data comes from the Muster and Descriptive Books and from the pension records cited elsewhere in this paper. See also the 1860 Census and Julia Floyd Smith, *Slavery and Plantation Growth in Antebellum Florida* (Gainesville, University of Florida Press, 1973), 25-26.

Eartha White Collection,
University of North Florida Library.

Albert Sammis, born a slave on a plantation near Jacksonville, became Col. Thomas W. Higginson's orderly.

in some form of agricultural enterprise. Ten percent were employed in skilled crafts: 12 were carpenters, two were machinists, two were tailors, one was a shoemaker, and one was a bricklayer. Two volunteers, both free men before the war, were employed as engineers. Regional economic activities beyond agriculture were also reflected in the men's prior occupations: 14 men gave teamster, draymen, wagoneer, hosteler or coachman as their occupations, while nine said they had been lumbermen or sawyers, and 12 said they were boatmen or sailors. Fifty-seven said they had been cooks, waiters or servants, reflecting that they came from towns in the region that drew business and tourist travellers even before 1861. From St. Augustine alone came 25 waiters and three cooks.[57]

The three loyal regiments from South Carolina were often on duty in northeast Florida. Higginson's first expedition into Florida came in January 1863 in the form of a raid up the St. Marys River on a mission to carry the Emancipation Proclamation into the interior, to plunder lumber mills, ransack the countryside and gain needed supplies. It was a highly successful mission although one member of the Second Florida Cavalry called it a "general thieving expedition." Following a skirmish in which the Confederates were forced to withdraw a Southern soldier later wrote: "What makes it more maddening is they are all nigger soldiers, officered by white men."[58]

The St. Marys River raid convinced General Saxton to send Higginson and his black troops up the St. Johns. Saxton wrote: "I have reliable information that there are large numbers of able-bodied negroes in that vicinity who are watching for an opportunity to join us. The negroes from Florida are far more intelligent than any I have yet seen. . . . They will fight with as much desperation as any people in the world."[59]

The Second South Carolina recruited heavily at refugee camps at Beaufort, Hilton Head, and at the Florida locations of Jacksonville, Magnolia, Key West, and Fernandina. Col. James Montgomery, commander of the Second South Carolina, recruited his first two companies exclusively at Key West where numerous northeast Florida refugees had congregated. From Key West in early March 1863 Montgomery took his "raw recruits" north where he said they received their military training "at the mouth of the St. Johns River where they were allowed to fire a few shots to get used to their guns."[60]

On March 9, 1863, the First and Second South Carolina regiments

57. *Ibid.*

58. W. Stephens to O. Stephens, 8 February 1863; D. Bryant to W. Bryant, 14 Feb. 1863. For an account of the St. Mary's raid see Higginson, 84-90.

59. Saxton to Stanton, 6 March 1863, ORA I: 14, 423.

60. Col. James Montgomery to Mrs. George Stearns, 25 April 1863, Papers of George Luther Stearns and Mary Elizabeth Stearns, MSS 171, Kansas State Historical Society, Topeka. Montgomery's letters, in the James Montgomery Collection at the same library, make it clear that he shared Higginson's devotion to abolition.

arrived off the mouth of the St. Johns, waiting until 2 A. M. on the 10th before starting upriver for Jacksonville under a bright moon. As they approached the city the Florida men became, in Higginson's words, "wild with delight" and called out in their "favorite phrase, 'too much good' . . ."[61]

To the surprise of everyone, the occupation of Jacksonville by the First South Carolina on March 10 occurred without a shot in opposition. There were about 500 civilians living in the town at the time. Most were whites who regarded this third occupation by their former slaves to be the "last crowning humiliation" in their wartime experiences. The black soldiers were insulted and sworn at, particularly by the ladies of the town, according to Higginson. After claiming to be in "perpetual fear" and demanding to be allowed to leave the city, several hundred people were evacuated in one 48-hour period.[62]

Some white residents had good reason to fear for their personal safety. Hattie Reed was startled to see a soldier who had only recently been the property of her father. She wrote to a family friend that Jake had returned a "bold soldier boy" after escaping to a Union gunboat in October 1862. Jake went looking for Hattie's father, banker and planter A. M. Reed, immediately after arriving, threatening to take vengeance on him for selling Etta to buyers somewhere in Georgia. Hattie said that Jake wanted "to meet Pa face to face to teach him what it is to part man and wife." Jake also put a gun to the head of a man who had helped deter the prior runaway attempt of the Reed slaves. A. M. Reed was so frightened, Hattie said, that he would not stay at his home at Mulberry Grove at night, and was seldom there during the day. "We are moving away as many things as possible," she said. Later, when Jake was overheard threatening to burn the Reeds' home, he was arrested and confined for the duration of the Union occupation.[63]

Another slave owner savored the return of his former chattels, writing: "Our negro Ted was among the troops at Jacksonville, also Mrs. Duval's boy Henry. Henry was mortally wounded in one of their skirmishes and has since died. So out of five who left our plantation last year only two are well and strong. . . . Does this not seem a just retribution?"[64]

Higginson realized that many of his men "had private wrongs to avenge," but he kept a tight discipline, all the while marveling that only rarely did they give visible signals of a desire for revenge. He later wrote: "I shall never forget the self-control with which one of our best sergeants pointed out to me, at Jacksonville, the very place where one of his brothers had been hanged by the whites for leading a party of

61. Higginson, 97.

62. *Ibid.*, 115-116. See also W. Stephens to O. Stephens, 16 March 1863.

63. Hattie Reed to D. Bryant 22 March 1863; O. Stephens to D. Bryant 2 April 1863. Bryant-Stephens Collection

64. Anonymous to Loulie Tydings, 4 April 1863, Bryant-Stephens Collection.

National Archives.

Col. Thomas W. Higginson used the John P. Sanderson house in Jacksonville for his headquarters.

fugitive slaves. He spoke of it as a historic matter, without any bearing on the present issue."[65]

While the First South Carolina held Jacksonville against Confederate forays during the third occupation, Colonel Montgomery's incomplete regiment took part in minor skirmishes; within 24 hours they were under heavy attack. For the next several weeks they undertook assignments throughout the area, recruiting heavily in the field to fill the ranks of their new regiment. Higginson best described Montgomery's forays:

> In Colonel Montgomery's hands these up-river raids reached the dignity of a fine art. His conceptions of foraging were rather more Western and liberal than mine, and on these excursions he fully indemnified himself for any undue abstinence demanded of him when in camp. I remember being on the wharf, with some naval officers, when he came down from his first trip. The steamer seemed an animated hen-coop. Live poultry hung from the foremast shrouds, dead ones from the mainmast, geese hissed from the binnacle, a pig paced the quarter deck, and a duck's wings were seen fluttering from a line which was wont to sustain duck trousers.[66]

These raids were anything but amusing to Finegan. "They are robbing and plundering everything on the east bank," Finegan wrote, ". . . [and probably plan] to occupy Jacksonville with white troops and send the negroes . . . to Palatka and then attempt to move amongst the plantations."[67]

On March 27, Montgomery and 120 black troops started on an expedition upriver toward Palatka, raiding plantations along the way. Thomas T. Russell, a local planter, reported that at least six landings were made and that the black troops carried off slaves, horses, carts, poultry, hogs, cotton, salt—"everything else they could lay their hands upon."[68] As a result of Montgomery's raids the Second South Carolina mustered in numerous northeast Florida men. These were exactly the kinds of developments that Abraham Lincoln had hoped for. On learning of the northeast Florida troops' activites Lincoln wrote to General Hunter: "I am glad to see the accounts of your colored force at Jacksonville. . . . I see the enemy are driving at them fiercely, as is to be expected. It is important to the enemy that such a force shall not take shape and grow and thrive in the South, and in precisely the same proportion it is important to us that it shall."[69]

65. Higginson, 236.
66. *Ibid.*, 120.
67. Finegan to Brig. Gen. Thomas Jordan, 14 March 1863, ORA I: 14, 226-9.
68. *Ibid.*, Russell to Finegan, 2 April 1863, 860-1.
69. Pres. Abraham Lincoln to Maj. Gen. D. Hunter, 1 April 1863, in John G. Nicolay and John Hay, *Abraham Lincoln; Complete Works* (New York, Century Co., 1902), II: 321.

On the one point, Lincoln and Finegan were in agreement. Shaken by the "celerity and secrecy" by which the "Abolition troops" had taken Jacksonville, Finegan immediately ordered troops from around Florida to concentrate to the west to check Federal progress into the interior. "To do this," he wrote, "I am compelled to leave with entirely inadequate protection many important points on the coast where negroes may escape in large numbers to the enemy and where they have easy access to the interior."[70] Recognizing that once again freedom was as close as the St. Johns River, Finegan warned the Confederate command that a means to hold the river must be found or else the entire slave population would be lost. Finegan was ready to predicate Confederate policy in Florida on retaining the vital black workers. He wired Richmond the following warning:

> the entire negro population of East Florida will be lost and the country ruined . . . unless the means of holding the St. Johns River are immediately supplied. . . . To appreciate the danger of the permanent establishment of these posts of negro troops on the St. Johns River I respectfully submit to the commanding general that a consideration of the topography of the country will exhibit the fact that the entire planting interest of East Florida lies within easy communication of the river; that intercourse will immediately commence between negroes on the plantations and those in the enemy's service, that this intercourse will suffice to corrupt the entire slave population of East Florida.[71]

Well aware of Confederate reactions to his black troops, General Saxton informed Secretary of War Stanton: "The Negroes are collecting in Jacksonville from all quarters."[72] Saxton was convinced that "scarcely an incident in this war has caused a greater panic throughout the whole Southern coast than this raid of the colored troops in Florida." In tallying the successes of the mission, Saxton could cite that the ranks of the two regiments had been augmented by in-the-field recruiting, that the occupation had received extensive coverage in the Northern press, and that white and black troops had served together for the first time during the war.[73]

Despite these successes the Union command decided to terminate the third occupation of Jacksonville. The troop transports steamed back to Beaufort carrying battle-tested veterans alongside raw recruits.

70. Finegan to Jordan, 14 March 1863, ORA I: 14, 227-8.

71. *Ibid.*, 229.

72. Saxton to Stanton, 14 March 1863, ORA I: 14, 227.

73. For discussion of the third occupation of Jacksonville and the tragic fire set by arsonists as the troop transports were loading see Martin and Schafer, ch. 5. For discussion of the Northern newspapers see Richard A. Martin, "The *New York Times* Views Civil War Jacksonville," *Florida Historical Quarterly*, 53 (April 1975).

Fernandina's burgeoning black refugee camps swelled to over 15,000 following the evacuation of Jacksonville, prompting Col. Milton S. Littlefield to recruit the first 101 volunteers for the Third South Carolina from the refugee ranks.[74]

The First and Third South Carolina regiments continued fighting for freedom in South Carolina until the war ended. The Second South Carolina came back to Jacksonville in February 1864 and took part in the tragic battle of Olustee, suffering heavy casualties alongside black and white regiments from the North. Following Olustee the regiment stayed in Jacksonville, continuing its earlier pattern of raiding plantations for supplies and recruits.[75]

On September 4, 1864, for example, Col. William R. Noble led men from the Thirty-fourth (the Second Carolina before mustered into regular service), the Thirty-fifth and the One-hundred-second United States Colored Infantry, and white troops of the Ohio Mounted Infantry, and the Third Rhode Island Artillery on a four-day raid from Magnolia (present-day Green Cove Springs) to the north of Lake George. The previous day, Dr. Esther Hill Hawks witnessed the concluding scenes of a mass runaway phenomenon: 30 black refugees were seen south of Magnolia on the banks of the St. Johns River. They waved a flag until one of the gunboats picked them up and carried them to freedom in Jacksonville.[76]

The military record of the loyal South Carolina regiments is largely admirable. By escaping they had passed a test of courage; for the lure of freedom some would-be escapees paid with their lives at the hands of Confederate troops and vigilantes. Not content to have broken their personal chains of slavery, they joined the United States Army and fought for the freedom of others, knowing that the Union government paid them substantially less each month than it paid the white soldiers.

The black troops also knew that they and their white officers were subject to execution by Confederate authorities if captured and detained as prisoners of war, and that they would probably be re-enslaved if the Union cause failed. "They had more to fight for than the whites," Colonel Higginson felt: "Besides the flag and the Union, they had home and wife and child. They fought with ropes round their necks."[77]

74. Calvin Robinson, "Ms of Robinson concerning his residence in Jacksonville during the Civil War," MS Box 51, P. K. Yonge Library.

75. See Cornish, *The Sable Arm*; Higginson, *Army Life*. See the letters Montgomery wrote to his wife, especially 25, 29, 30, 31 August 1863, concerning the seige of Fort Wagner, in James Montgomery Collection, Kansas State Historical Society, Topeka. Also helpful are Frederick H. Dyer, *A Compendium of the War of the Rebellion*, III, and *Official Register, Volunteer Forces, United States Army, 1861-1865*, VIII.

76. Col. William R. Noble to J. P. Hatch, 4 September 1864, MS Box 4, P. K. Yonge Library. Gerald Schwartz, ed., *A Woman Doctor's Civil War: Esther Hill Hawks' Diary* (University of South Carolina Press, 1984), 77. See also Gerald Schwartz, "An Integrated Free School in Civil War Florida," *Florida Historical Quarterly*, LXI (October 1982). The Library of Congress has an extensive collection of letters between Esther Hawks and her husband, John Milton Hawks, a surgeon with the USCI.

77. Higginson, 237.

Pvt. Thomas Long, a northeast Florida man serving in the First South Carolina, captured in a brief speech the spirit of the slave runaways that joined Union forces. Speaking to the regiment as lay chaplain for the day, Private Long said that becoming soldiers had been an act of liberation that had helped prepare them for American citizenship.

> If we hadn't become sojers, all might have gone back as it was before; our freedom might have slipped through two houses of Congress and President Linkum's four years might have passed by and notin' been done for us. But now tings can neber go back, because we have showed our energy and our courage and our naturally manhood.
>
> Anoder ting is, suppose you had kep your freedom witout enlisting in dis army; your children might have growed up free and been well cultivated . . . but it would have been always flung in dere faces—'Your fader never fought for he own freedom'—and what could day answer? Neber can say dat to dis African Race no more.[78]

Private Long settled in Jacksonville after being discharged from the army, becoming a preacher and eventually serving three terms in the Florida Senate.

Many other veterans of the loyal South Carolina regiments came back to northeast Florida after the war, settling in the towns and farms of the region. These veterans entered civilian life with a rudimentary education intended by their abolitionist tutors to prepare them for a life of responsible citizenship. Throughout the fourth occupation of Jacksonville which began February 7, 1864, hundreds of black soldiers attended the flourishing "free school" run by Dr. Esther Hawks and the American Missionary Society. Dr. Hawks began teaching the men of the First South Carolina in Beaufort on January 15, 1863. Following the February 1864 occupation of Jacksonville she founded another free school there. It was racially integrated at first, and Dr. Hawks was a teacher during the spring 1864 and 1864-65 school terms.

Some of the veterans joined in a communal farming venture on the northern outskirts of Jacksonville founded by a surgeon with the Second South Carolina, Dr. Daniel Dustin Hanson. Leasing or selling plots to soldiers and other black families, Hanson also helped the freedmen market their crops and pool their earnings for further land purchases. Today, this section of Jacksonville is still known as Hansontown.[79]

---

78. *Ibid.*, 19-20. For Long's postwar life see his pension record; Theresa Dive, ed. "The Black Facts Handbook," University of North Florida History Committee (1985), 14-15; and Jerrell H. Shofner, *Nor Is It Over Yet: Florida in the Era of Reconstruction, 1863-1887* (Gainesville, University Presses of Florida, 1974), 143.

79. Daniel D. Hanson, pension record 362.152, RG 94.

Library of Congress.

Esther Hill Hawks as a young woman.

Hanson later joined with Colonel William W. Marple and Lt. Colonel William L. Apthorp, both of the Second South Carolina, in a purchase of several thousand acres of land in what became known as Arlington for the establishment of a larger communal settlement for freedmen. Little is known about the fate of the colony, other than that it failed.[80]

Evidence in the military pension records indicates that most black veterans from the region made individual adjustments to postwar life that were characterized by occupational diversity. South Carolina-born Henry Allen mustered out of the Second South Carolina and settled in Jacksonville and later in Pablo Beach, working variously as a laborer, oysterman, fisherman, raftsman, and porter in a store. Silas Forman made his living snaring rattlesnakes and milking their venom for home remedies. David Hall became a drayman, William Johnson became a farmer at Chaseville, and Henry Adams returned to Jacksonville to resume his work in area sawmills. William Josey had been a carpenter before the war but became a mechanic after, while James Lang settled in Fernandina as a grocer, oysterman and carpenter. William Pappy returned to St. Augustine to work as a barber. Charles Wilson cut timber across northeast Florida, Simon Primus returned to the Mandarin area as an agricultural laborer, and James Lain worked as a blacksmith. Charles Knabb returned to Nassau County and became a successful cotton farmer and agent for a wealthy landowner. Thomas Holzendorf forsook the life of shoemaker and farmer in Kings Ferry for the life of a preacher. Harry Tillman and Smart Tillman invested in stock in Union surgeon John Milton Hawks' Florida Land and Lumber Company, destined for a short lifespan at Port Orange in Volusia County.[81]

Veterans who had been free men before 1861 also returned to northeast Florida, many to jobs not unlike those they had worked at before the war. Henry Hannahan of Pablo Beach resumed his life on the area waterways, working as a steward on the steamer *Dictator*. Alonzo H. Phillips returned to Jacksonville to work once again as a merchant. Later, he farmed at Chaseville. Lewis McQueen found employment as a mason in Jacksonville. Lewis Forester and his wife Affa went back to Magnolia to the same farm they had worked before the Yankee gunboats came upriver in 1862. Nearby, George Floyd farmed a piece of land on the St. Johns opposite Black Creek. Samuel Osborn II had been a waiter in St. Augustine; after the war he settled in Savannah, working as a waiter at the Pulaski House, before returning to St. Augustine in 1884.[82]

By fall 1865 black veterans in Jacksonville had organized a series of public meetings to discuss the needs of the poor in the community, and

80. *Ibid.*

81. See John Milton Hawks, "Prospectus of the Florida Land and Lumber Company," MS Box 3, No. 2, P. K. Yonge Library.

82. See pension records cited in notes 18-20.

had decided to purchase a farm outside the town to use as a home for the aged and infirm. Other issues discussed were education and the rights and duties of black citizens. On September 22, 1865, the *Jacksonville Herald* reported that black soldiers were planning to exert pressures via petitions to gain the right of suffrage. During Reconstruction many of the veterans participated actively in the affairs of the Republican Party, some filling appointive and elective offices.[83]

These trained soldiers, veterans of bloody battles throughout the southeast, possessers of rudimentary educations and an expectation that they were to become equal citizens of the nation soon after the guns stopped firing, would not acquiesce easily to the white supremacist politics that came to Jacksonville soon after the war. The extent to which their lives reflected a spirit of "hope and encouragement" is worthy of a separate study, one that could benefit from perusal of the military pension records kept in the National Archives and the parts they played in the dramatic events of the immediate postwar years would be an interesting sequel for researchers concerned with the few successes and many failures of the Reconstruction years.

---

83. *Jacksonville Herald*, 1, 22 September 1865.

Researching the Civil War in Florida: An Introduction to the Southern Historical Collection

Everard H. Smith

Professional historians concentrating on the Civil War are frequently asked whether there is really anything new to discover about it. It is easy to see why the question arises. The Late Unpleasantness has been examined, analyzed—and occasionally re-fought—more intensely than any comparable period in American history. The volume of literature is simply staggering, and even today, nearly a century and a quarter after its close, the flow of new articles and books seems never ending. Given this situation, one might readily conclude that eager historians had long since devoured every scrap of relevant information in sight.

Surprisingly enough, despite generations of scrutiny, the source material of the Civil War is far from exhausted today. Much of it remains unexplored in the unpublished letters, diaries, and personal papers of participants. These records, which exist by the hundreds of thousands, have been gathered at archives throughout the nation, where they constitute a resource whose potential is still largely untapped. While manuscripts can be used to highlight detail or to provide new insight into old topics, their chief value lies in their documentation of ordinary lives and events not described in history books. Where published material is scanty or nonexistent, they are often the only form of substantiation possible.

One great manuscript repository is the Southern Historical Collection at the University of North Carolina at Chapel Hill, a mecca for Southern scholars since its establishment six decades ago. Its holdings, currently estimated at 8,000,000 documents, cover the region's history from colonial times to the present. The Collection is an institution with which everyone who studies the South should be familiar. Archival research there, in the wartime years of Saint Augustine and Florida, could well be productive.

The Collection is the product of the pioneering vision of Professor J. G. de Roulhac Hamilton (1878-1961), a native North Carolinian who joined the faculty of the state university in 1906. As early as the 1920's, Hamilton was fired with the idea of creating, in his own words, "a center of unique character, [which] will make possible research for the first time in problems of a region in the midst of economic and social revolution. Never has there been a time when the preservation and the study

---

Everard H. Smith is a research fellow and visiting lecturer in history at the University of North Carolina at Chapel Hill. He is a former staff member of the Southern Historical Collection, and a specialist in primary source material from the Civil War period.

of its history . . . were more important and when they could contribute more splendidly, not only in securing for the South its rightful place in national history, but also in making available information that will be of the highest practical value in its economic and cultural development."[1]

Although related by birth to many of the "first families" of the South—a fact which he did not hesitate to exploit in his collecting—Hamilton's orientation toward history was free from elitism. This foresight was all the more remarkable in an era when Southern history was still dominated by tales of rich plantation owners and dashing cavalry generals. To Hamilton, however, any document was valuable regardless of its humble origins, and he made strenuous efforts to seek out the papers of "plain folk" as well as of the wealthy or famous.

Under Hamilton's constant prodding, the university established the Southern Historical Collection in 1930. Thereafter, with missionary zeal, he embarked on a lifetime of collecting that made him legendary. He roamed the South in a Model A Ford, rescuing papers from attics, cellars, carriage houses, and—in one memorable instance—a chicken coop. A cultured, entertaining conversationalist, he usually gained his donors' confidence without trouble, although it is recorded that he once angered an elderly Savannah matron by speaking kind words about Gen. William Tecumseh Sherman. (Shifting gears rapidly, he saved the situation by remarking that he was certain Sherman was now burning in hell.) Envious critics began calling him J. G. de Ransack Hamilton, and even threatened him with legal action to try to halt the steady stream of papers to Chapel Hill. But by his retirement in 1948 he had amassed over 2,000,000 documents, a total that has since quadrupled under three subsequent directors.

Today the collection has amply fulfilled its founder's dream. It enjoys an international reputation, and welcomes thousands of researchers annually. It contains more than 4,000 separate groups of papers, most of them acquired by donation or by contributions from a large circle of enthusiastic benefactors. The majority of these groups have no restrictions on their access or use. They may be viewed by any visitor with proper identification and a legitimate historical research interest. A few groups carry restrictions imposed by the original donors or their descendants.

When a new manuscript group arrives at the collection, it is first given an identifying number and named for the people or places most prominent in it. Next, conservation measures are undertaken—a matter of serious concern, since many paper products contain acidic ingredients that cause eventual deterioration. The papers are then arranged in chronological order, stored in acid-free containers, and housed in a fire-

1. Quoted by J. Carlyle Sitterson, "The Southern Historical Collection, 1930-1980: The Pursuit of History," in *The Bookmark: Fiftieth Anniversary, Southern Historical Collection* (Chapel Hill, 1981), 47.

proof environment where temperature and humidity levels are carefully controlled.

Meanwhile, staff members prepare the various finding aids that comprise the heart of the collection. A comprehensive card catalogue is divided into proper name, geographic, and subject headings. Detailed inventories, indexed to the card catalogue, describe the group folder by folder and, in a few cases, item by item. In addition, a published *Guide* (1970) and *Supplementary Guide* (1976) provide brief summaries of the inventories, usually a single paragraph long.

Although archivists make every effort to describe the contents of manuscripts thoroughly, it is evident that they cannot anticipate every way in which an individual item might prove useful. Hence, finding aids are normally only a starting point for archival research. While there is no guarantee of ultimate success, patient investigation is often rewarded with valuable discoveries among unindexed papers, or in materials whose significance had been overlooked. Scholars are thus encouraged to visit the collection personally to experience the joy of discovery, or to engage a private researcher if they are unable to make the trip. Staff members will gladly answer written inquiries concerning sources, potential topics, or general information, but they cannot do research for correspondents. Prospective visitors should write in advance to the Southern Historical Collection, University of North Carolina, Wilson Library 024-A, Chapel Hill, North Carolina 27514. Copies of current information forms and the two published guides are available at the St. Augustine Historical Society's library. The *Guide* and *Supplementary Guide* may also be ordered by mail from the Southern Historical Collection for $7.00 and $2.50 separately, or $9.00 together.

Finally, what may we say of the manuscripts themselves? The published guides, which in turn are merely an introduction to the collection, reveal that at least forty groups pertain to the history of Florida between 1861 and 1865. If these dates are extended backward into the antebellum period, or forward into Reconstruction, the total goes much higher. No brief description can characterize such a diverse set of materials. A few of these papers relate to prominent figures such as Stephen R. Mallory, Confederate secretary of the navy, and Gen. Edmund Kirby Smith. But the majority concern Florida backwoods farmers, townspeople, merchants, housewives, common soldiers, slaves.

The stories these manuscripts relate are as varied as the Southern experience itself. Dr. David Winchester Whitehurst, whose records may be found in group #4057, was a Saint Augustine physician active in the American Colonization Society. Following the war he nursed prisoners during the famous yellow fever epidemic at Fort Jefferson. Alonzo B. Noyes (#3166) was the Federal lighthouse superintendent and customs collector at Saint Marks until April, 1861. William Louis Criglar (#1196) ran a lumber mill in Escambia County which employed slave labor as late as 1862. The crew of the *Oneida*, a blockader stationed off Pensacola, kept an informal daily log of their activities (#3171). The Confederate defenses opposing them onshore were engineered in part by Col. Samuel Henry Lockett (#432); his papers include six rare photographs taken there in 1861 by New Orleans photographer J. D. Edwards. The list could be extended indefinitely. Some of these documents are written in polished prose and elegant penmanship that would put a modern college graduate to shame. Others are barely legible. Whatever their origins, they all add additional tiles to a complex mosaic.

Generally speaking, the manuscript records will be searched in vain if one is looking for heroes, villains, high drama, or graphic eyewitness reports of battles reeking with blood and victory. What will be found instead is the commonplace fabric of everyday existence—the ideals, values, family relationships, business affairs, mundane struggles, and petty crises of life—recorded for the most part by prosaic people who had no idea that their activities would some day fascinate a future audience. The researcher is swept back into the past, enabled for a moment to stand directly in a predecessor's footsteps, knowing only what he knew, learning only as he learned. No other form of artifact offers such immediacy, such total identification with times long gone. Shelby Foote, an acclaimed novelist and Civil War scholar, had high praise for the Southern Historical Collection: "When I began writing history, I began to understand that an historian may have many ways of dealing with the subject he has chosen. He may want to explain along the way what is happening and the various choices that obtain; or he may, and this is my preference, try to show you what people are rather than try to explain them. . . . Stark questions occur when you begin to deal with certain moments. One of the most dramatic of these moments is Pickett's Charge, and if you go to Gettysberg and stand by the Lee monument and look across to Cemetery Ridge, you will see a long rolling valley about a mile wide, totally exposed from the step-off point to the crest of the far ridge. There were about 12,000 men marching across that valley where cannon balls were bowling along and, when they got close enough, rifle bullets were whizzing. And you wonder what kind of a man will make that walk. . . . You begin to realize that if you are going to tell that story, you have to understand why those men crossed that valley.

"There are many reasons. Their religion was one strong element in it, their family pride, their regimental pride (probably the strongest of all), their pride in their new nation, their belief in their commander, R. E. Lee. All of these elements go into making it up, and how well you define them is determined by the extent of your familiarity with certain documents preserved in repositories such as the Southern Historical Collection. You go back to the records of the plantations; you study about their relationships with the people they worked for. You begin to find what their home life was like, and a good historian, having found those things, will put them in his text so that a person reading about Pickett's Charge will not say, 'How in God's name could they go across that valley?' He will know how they could go across that valley, because he will have become acquainted with the elements that went into their makeup. And it is in the Southern Historical Collection that you will find the answers to these things."[2]

MANUSCRIPT GROUPS OF PARTICULAR INTEREST TO THE STUDY OF THE CIVIL WAR IN FLORIDA

This list has been compiled from the descriptions in Susan S. Blosser and Clyde N. Wilson, *The Southern Historical Collection: A Guide to Manuscripts* (Chapel Hill, 1970); and Everard H. Smith, *The Southern Historical Collection: Supplementary Guide to Manuscripts* (Chapel Hill, 1976). For full details, consult these two publications. This list should not be regarded as comprehensive.

38 James B. Bailey Papers
62 Overton and Jesse Bernard Diaries
80 Joseph Branch Papers
245 Mrs. Nicholas Ware Eppes Papers
276 Jeremy Francis Gilmer Papers
332 Hentz Family Papers
404 Edmund Kirby-Smith Papers
425 Edward McCrady L'Engle Papers
432 Samuel Henry Lockett Papers
440 Washington J. Lutterloh Papers
529 Raphael J. Moses Autobiography
551 George Sidney Thompson Confederate Quartermaster Records
643 Ruffin, Roulhac, and Hamilton Family Papers
655 Henry C. Semple Papers
664 Leah and Rebecca Simpson Papers
723 William Victor Tomb and James Harvey Tomb Papers
972 James Jones Philips Papers
991 Tench Tilghman Diary
1159 Lucy (Wood) Butler Papers
1186 Stephen R. Mallory Papers
1196 William Louis Criglar Papers
1253 S. S. Alderman Photograph
1404 Henry Summer Paper
1525 Wilmot Stuart Holmes Collection
1704 Wirt Family Papers

2. Shelby Foote, "The Southern Historical Collection," *Ibid.*, 70-71.

1738 Allen Turner Davidson Letters
1826 John Parkhill Papers
2420 Milner Family Papers
2560 Joseph B. Cumming Recollections
2718 Branch Family Papers
2747 William Frederick Penniman Reminiscences
2943 Florida Railroad Map
3166 Alonzo B. Noyes Papers
3171 *Oneida* Ship Diary
3267 Joseph Dill Alison Diary
3273 Pensacola & Georgia Railroad Account Book
3723 William Henry Boyce Letters
4057 Weedon and Whitehurst Family Papers
4065 James H. Stanley Papers
4074 Samuel Hilton Steelman Collection